A Surprise from the Sea

How Hudson the Cat Became a Cruise Ship Captain

Emma Le Teace

Jerome Vincent

Brilliant Books

First published in paperback by Brilliant Books 2024

Text © Emma Le Teace & Jerome Vincent

Illustrations by Irfan Budhiharjo

Emma Le Teace and Jerome Vincent assert their moral right to be identified as the authors of this work.

ISBN 978-1-9173280-0-5

Captain Hudson Copyright / Registered

Britishism:

Brilliant – Something that is really, really great. It doesn't have to be clever, just enjoyable or simply wonderful.

1.

And it all started... in the sea, one late windy afternoon on Brighton's famous pebble beach.

Emma was walking along watching the Sun as it thought about setting itself.

It looked like it was just hanging there, hesitant, undecided; "Can I be bothered to go around the world yet again?" the Sun seemed to be saying to itself.

Emma laughed.

The Earth goes around the Sun, silly!

Then it struck her that if the *Earth* was being lazy, then that might be bad news for...

Everyone ON the Earth!

Because if our planet slowed down or even stopped turning then...

Emma didn't know what would happen then. If it did happen, well it might be...

don't say it – The End of The World!

That would be inconvenient.

VERY inconvenient.

Why? Because Emma was dreaming about going to sea once more. You see, she had just come back from a cruise on a really big, a REALLY BIG...

GIGANTIC cruise ship.

All her friends had told her she would hate it.

It's full of OLD PEOPLE

You'll get SEASICK

You'll FALL OVER BOARD

A WHALE will SWALLOW you

No! A SHARK will eat you

It'll SINK like the TITANIC

You'll be so BORED, you'll come back and even enjoy MATHS!

Well, Emma took no notice. None of those warnings had any effect (although she was a little scared of getting seasick – but didn't usually) and, besides, she positively *loved* maths.

> **Britishism: *Maths* – math in the US. 'Mathematics' is a plural word, really.**

And the cruise itself turned out to be as good as she thought it would.

She loved it: Being at sea, the big wide sea. The most tantalising, surprising, perplexing thing she'd ever experienced.

The sea, the sea, the sea.

Wait a minute...

There's something orange bobbing in the sea.

Emma blinked, then strained her eyes, but she couldn't see what it was.

For a moment it looked like a cat – a kitten to be exact.

Emma went back to thinking about the sea, and how she longed to go back. To sea. On a ship. A great big cruise ship with lots to do, not just for grown-ups, but for kids too. All kinds of kids of ALL ages.

Her voyage had come to an end and Emma was back on land. Her mum had said she'd get her *sea legs* quick enough, but Emma had got them instantly.

Britishism: *Mum* **is 'mom' – strangely it used to be how people in England's midlands said it centuries ago.**

It was as if she'd been *born* to go to sea.

Now on land, she felt... - nothing. No movement. No depth. Just... - land.

Right now that meant damp pebbles. Behind her was the famous Brighton Pier, stretching out into the grey-blue water. She didn't want to go on it. Some people said that walking to the end of the pier was like going out to sea. She'd tried and it wasn't. You couldn't feel the waves through the soles of your feet.

Err, that orange shape – which might be a cat or a kitten… is getting closer.

Emma really wished the land would move like the sea. Though, if it did then that might be bad. It could be an earthquake. And Earthquakes were bad. But in Brighton, on the south coast of England, earthquakes never happened.

Emma hoped so, at least.

She sighed. The Sun had decided it was time to get ready to set at last…

Or, no… to be more precise, the *Earth* had changed its mind about not completing its daily turn around the block.

That's when she realised that the orange shape she was seeing, the one bobbing up and down in the water – or maybe on the water – was…

An orange circular thing with a furry orange blob standing on it.

Emma squinted. Sometimes doing that helped her see further. It was like turning her eyes into binoculars. And, although it's impossible to actually make your eyes zoom in on anything, she managed to make out that this orange shape *was* a cat…

Which was strange.

A cat in the water appearing out of nowhere!

A very strange thing to happen

Out of the blue!

Actually, not a strange *single* thing – but a strange *combination* of two things you wouldn't normally see together.

A lifebelt and a -- she still couldn't believe it.

Could it really be?

Yes, it really was.

A cat!

Now it was close, she could see that it *was* a kitten. An actual kitten.

Emma squinted and turned her eyes into binoculars

A kitten!?

At sea!?

On a lifebelt!?

Emma told her mind to drop all the annoying exclamation marks and focus on what she needed to do.

And that was, simply...

Rescue that cat!

Kitten!

Orange thing!

She stepped forward, the pebbles clacking and crunching as she carefully made her way to the edge of the swishing waves that flowed forward and then fell back with a very wet squelching sound.

As the life belt and its orange cargo bobbed closer, Emma could see that the cat – the kitten – didn't look distressed, afraid, or sad but... happy.

Emma watched as the waves carried the lifebelt and the kitten closer and closer.

Britishism: *Lifebelt* **– known as a life preserver in the US**

On her cruise, Emma met some American children who had been confused by some of the words she'd used, like 'lifebelt' instead of 'life preserver'. And Emma had been confused by some of the words *they'd* used. She'd always thought that English was what they spoke in the United States. But

11

their version was different to Emma's version in some strange ways. Ways that amused her.

Hold on! Why am I thinking of Britishisms!

At a time like this!

When a kitten has just appeared out of the wide blue sea!

She clicked her mind back to the lifebelt and the kitten clinging to it, which had finally wedged itself between two small mounds of pebbles.

Emma expected the kitten to jump off straight away and run for its life, but it didn't. It just sat there. It looked at Emma and seemed to examine her closely. It was taking in every detail of her face, her hair, her coat, and her shoes. At that point it frowned and said, "Your shoes are getting wet."

As she looked down, Emma saw that the kitten was right. Her were, indeed, getting wet. Not too wet, but wet enough to annoy her mother when she got home...

Wait a minute!

The kitten just spoke to me!

Emma didn't want to frighten the kitten away by screaming or jumping back in surprise or looking like she'd just seen a ghost or something equally scary, so she worked hard to stay calm even though inside she was definitely NOT calm!

So, she just stood there, staring at the talking kitten sitting on an orange lifebelt on a pebbly beach, at sunset, after floating in out of the blue… *literally*.

"My name's Hudson, and it is my ambition to be the captain of a cruise ship. I am very, very pleased to meet you."

2.

"I'm not orange, I'm ginger," Hudson said frankly as Emma cradled him in her arms trying to dry his fur and wipe off the sea salt. She'd made the mistake of remarking that he was 'a lovely little orange kitten,' but Hudson had objected.

He also corrected Emma when she said, "It was lucky I was here on the beach so I could rescue you."

"You're very kind, and yes, I am happy that you picked me up out of the water but, umm, rescued? That's going too far," Hudson was clearly a very self-confident little *ginger* kitten.

"But if I hadn't been here you might have drifted away... or got lost on the beach... or been picked up by someone nasty... or worse," Emma tried to explain.

You're very kind... but rescued? That's going too far.

3.

Hudson never did tell Emma the story.

Sometimes she'd try and coax it from him as they lay on the sofa watching TV programmes about the sea and all the amazing life in it. But he'd softly place his paw on her lips as if to say, "*Don't ask because I won't tell until it's the right time.*"

Emma wondered when the 'right time' would arrive. Might it be when he was fully grown? Or was he waiting for Emma to grow up? Or maybe he was waiting for a sign – some news from far away, or a mysterious visitor who would turn up at Emma's door dressed in a sou'wester (that's a heavy, oilskin raincoat mariners wear at sea) with a message in a bottle from...

A message in a bottle!?

A man in a sou'wester!?

You've been watching too many films and reading too many stories!

She was content to wait. Her mum had always told her that, "good things come to those who wait." So, she decided to be patient. When Hudson felt the time was right, he would tell the whole story of how he came to be in the sea on a life belt on that very special day.

Emma knew that meant watching Hudson grow into a strong, handsome cat, confident on the streets and in the gardens of the town in which her family lived. A cat who would become a leader of other cats in the neighbourhood, feared by some, admired by others.

Which is exactly what happened.

Grown-up Hudson always seemed to have a plan and a mission. He would slip nimbly through the cat-flap that Emma's Dad had made from parts he'd kept from an old washing machine. She'd watch as he gracefully jumped up onto the fence between their garden and the next-door neighbour's. He would place his feet carefully so that he was perfectly balanced. His four paws looked as if he was about to do a ballroom dance, and he would scan the horizon, sniff the air, and twist his ears left and right to check out what was happening across his domain.

Hudson became an important member of Emma's family almost instantly. Everyone loved him; Mum, Dad, even 'Little Brother.' Emma always called her younger brother '*Little* Brother' just to annoy him. He wasn't so little now, even though he *was* younger. But not by much.

One spring morning, two years after Hudson came into Emma's life, Mum announced that the family was going to go on another cruise. Emma was delighted and excited and then suddenly worried. A cruise? That meant going away for quite a long time. And that meant leaving Hudson behind. That was something she did not want to do, but she really, really wanted to go on a cruise again and be at sea, and she knew that there was no way to take Hudson with her. Pets are not allowed on a cruise ship. Not usually, anyway...

But... *BUT*...

BUT!

"And we're going on a brand new ship that allows you to bring your pets!" Mum said with a flourish because she knew exactly what Emma was thinking.

For a moment Emma thought she'd lost her hearing. Her head buzzed. She felt as though she was going to fall over. And then, just as Mum was repeating herself because Dad had said, "Whaaaaat!" Emma screamed...

"So Hudson can come!?"

"Yes, if he wants to, Hudson can come. It'll save us putting him into a cat hotel," Mum said.

"You mean a cattery!?" Emma exclaimed, with a tinge of horror in her voice. She didn't like the idea of ever putting Hudson in a cattery. Not because they weren't nice places – she was sure they were – but because if she went on holiday she wanted Hudson to come.

Britishism: *Cattery* – a place where cats are taken when their owners go on vacation. Same as kennels in the US.

"That's what I meant," Mum said, "but there's no need for a cattery because this ship is special! You can bring your pet!"

Emma looked at Hudson and Hudson looked at Emma. Usually, Emma never spoke out loud to Hudson like he could *actually* understand her when she was with her parents or other people, but this time she almost did.

Hudson put his paw to his mouth as if to say "*shhh, we'll talk about this later*" and Emma stopped herself from blurting out what she was absolutely dying to blurt out; that Hudson would absolutely *love* to go to sea because he wanted to become the captain of his own cruise liner one day. She knew this because he'd told her in *actual* words because – *Hudson can talk!*

But Mum and Dad you just don't know that he can!

He didn't want anyone but Emma to know that he could actually talk like a human. In fact, he could talk better than most humans. He always made sense. Most humans didn't. Not always.

So, Emma tried really hard not to let the cat - the *talking cat* – out of the bag. She sat very still and even though she looked like a balloon that had been blown up just a bit too much and was about to burst.

21

"Are you alright, Emma?" Mum asked. She was surprised by Emma's reaction to the news – the really good news – of the cruise.

Then Hudson jumped up onto the sofa and sat on Emma's lap. He did it to soothe her. To calm her down because he could see she was struggling to stay calm. It worked. Emma felt his warmth and the sound of his gentle purring helped her relax and stop looking like a balloon. He made her smile.

Their secret was safe. A new adventure was about to begin.

A new adventure was about to begin

4.

"What do you pack for a cat on a cruise?" Mum asked a few days before the family was to embark on their voyage.

Emma looked at Hudson who was looking quizzically at a scratching post that Dad had brought home from a Car Boot Sale.

Britishism: *Car Boot Sale* – **when British people sell stuff from the back of their cars (the** *'boot'* – **'trunk' in the US). Same as a garage or yard sale.**

Hudson's whiskers twitched as he examined what looked like something a kid had made out of three bits of wood and a few strips of rough carpet.

"Don't bring THAT, whatever you do!" Emma said.

Mum looked at the cat scratcher and smiled, "Your dad was trying his best, love. It says in the brochure that the kennels on the Pet Deck have everything a pet needs to keep occupied and have fun."

Emma had already packed her travel bag. It was ready for the voyage and sat by her bed. It had everything she would need on the ship. Her notebooks – one to write down the activities she would do onboard and one for the new friends she'd meet in the Kid's Club – and her special camera to take photos of... well...

EVERYTHING!

She wanted to take lots of pictures of Hudson in the kennels.

Kennels? But that's for dogs right?

Emma checked out the brochure for the cruise. It was big and glossy and full of great pictures of the ship and the sea.

The ship they were going on was called the *Magical Seas.* Emma loved that name. It described exactly what she felt; the seas *were* magical. And the sea was a magical place to be.

She leafed through the brightly coloured pages filled with pictures of the ship and the places it would call at. The first few days were 'sea days', when the ship would be just sailing on the ocean. That meant there'd be lots of time to get used to the ship and explore. And there was lots to explore!

Hudson sniffed at the brochure's glossy pages as Emma flicked through them, and then put his paw on the page that had pictures of the kennels and the cattery.

Ah! It has a cattery as well as kennels!

Emma was relieved. Hudson wasn't afraid of dogs. In fact, some of the dogs in Emma's neighbourhood were afraid of *him*. There was one yappy beagle that really annoyed Hudson because he always tried to jump up over the garden fence and chase Hudson. Luckily, the poor squat beagle was much too short to do it, and Hudson would watch with a look that said, "you're so weird."

It was a look that annoyed the beagle even more. It yapped and yapped until a slipper would fly out of the front door almost hitting him on his bottom. His owner was too lazy to ever take the beagle for a walk himself, so a kind neighbour took him out every day.

No, Hudson wasn't afraid of dogs, but he would prefer not to share his cruise with them. Emma nudged him to look down at the other pictures in the brochure.

"Look, you see?" She pointed at the pictures and Hudson followed her fingers as she flicked through the pages. "There's a cattery that's on the other side of the pets deck. It's actually called *The Pet Deck* – capital P and D – and it's up at the top on Deck 15. The cattery is one side, and the kennels are on the other. In between is a track where the dogs can go for a walk, and right in the middle of the deck are pet toys, and lots of things to scratch and play with. There's even a quiet place to snooze."

Emma and Hudson looked at the pictures in the brochure

Hudson liked a little snooze every afternoon, so he examined each of the pictures slowly and carefully. He was looking forward to going to sea. He hoped there wouldn't be too many dogs aboard and at least a few cats who might be interesting to talk to.

Reading the words below the pictures, Emma squealed with delight and read a sentence out loud to Hudson: "When the seas are calm enough, and with the permission of the Head Pet Officer, you may take your animal to your cabin once a day for a cosy visit."

Emma picked up Hudson and cuddled him. "You see! You can come and visit us in our cabin once a day! We can give you some of your favourite snacks!"

At the word 'snacks,' Hudson's ears twitched and became a little more pointed. He sniffed the pages and then nuzzled Emma's arm as she held the brochure open over her crossed legs.

Hudson loved a certain type of snack. They were called Temptys, and they were special treats made in all the flavours that cats like and which Hudson liked very, very much. When Emma even barely touched a packet of Temptys, Hudson's ears would prick up instantly, even if he was all the way down the garden. He'd sniff the air and then bound toward the cat-flap so he could have a few delicious, scrumptious, totally moreish Temptys.

"Oh," Emma frowned as she ran her finger over a small sentence that was printed in bold at the bottom of the page; it forbade passengers bringing their own food on board the ship. "We're not allowed to bring your Temptys onboard. Sorry, Hudson, no Temptys at sea for you."

Hudson was angry. For the first time since Dad had brought home the wonky cat scratcher, Hudson felt the urge to attack it with his claws.

Emma looked one way, and then another, and smiled as if she had thought of a plan. She leant down to whisper in Hudson's ear, "Don't worry, we'll be smugglers and get some Temptys on board somehow."

Hudson purred with gratitude and said, "But you hate breaking rules."

"Well, some rules are just meant to be broken," she whispered with a broad smile.

Emma closed the brochure and took a deep breath, "Now, let's get you packed. I've got you a special suitcase," She reached across her bedroom floor and pulled a small bag from under her bed. It looked like an old washbag. In fact, it was one.

Britishism: *Washbag* – a small waterproof bag you carry your toothbrush, soap, and facecloth in. In the US it's a 'Toiletry bag'

"This might *look* like an old washbag" she said, "but look..." Emma put it up close to Hudson's face, "I put cat stickers and Temptys stickers and wrote your name on it in five colours!"

Hudson looked at it as if to say, "Well, thanks but, I hardly need a bag of my own."

"Oh, you'll find it useful, you fussy old cat." Emma could read his looks perfectly by now. She thought his fussiness was amusing. Hudson was such a pernickety cat at times.

She started packing the bag. She put in a ball of wool, three plastic mice, and an old Christmas decoration of a reindeer with a bell around its neck and...

Hudson suddenly became alert as Emma took four packets of Temptys out of a shoebox. It was her secret stash, and they were all the flavours that Hudson loved. She wrapped them in a pair of her old pyjamas and put them at the bottom of the bag.

"We're all ready to set sail!" Emma called out to her parents and picked up Hudson and hugged him tight.

Little did they know that the voyage on *Magical Seas* would turn out to be the journey that would change their lives...

Forever.   *Forever*

For-EVER!

5.

Hudson was sat up straight in a special embarkation basket that the cruise line had given them when they arrived at Southampton, the port where they were to embark on their cruise. There was a big building called a Cruise Terminal, and passengers were getting out of cars and taxis and buses with lots of luggage. And pets. Pets on leads, in baskets, and cradled in eager children's arms.

Emma's mouth was hanging open as she stared upwards. Mum and Dad were standing behind them with the same awestruck looks on their faces.

Little Brother was picking his nose.

"Stop it!" Mum snapped when she finally spotted him doing it. "What will the other passengers think!?"

"They're too busy staring up at the ship," Emma said, her eyes still scanning from one side of the huge cruise ship to the other.

From the BOW to the STERN. From FORWARD to AFT. From the FRONT to the BACK.

It was a HUGE ship.

HUGE!

Huge and white with a long red stripe from one end to the other.

Its decks rose up into the sky like two skyscrapers on their sides. A big red and white funnel sat just beyond the middle of the top deck. Closer to the front was a mast and what looked like white footballs or balloons on stands. There were two sets of radar installations with spinning receivers linked to antennas. On either side of the mast a series of different coloured small flags fluttered in the breeze.

A long line of people were also staring up at the ship. Some passengers were already on board, and they waved down from the top decks as if to say, "Come on, it's wonderful and it's ready for you right now!"

"Got a pet? If you've got a pet of any kind, then join this line right here," said a man in a bright orange vest. He was tall and bald, and his face was very pale and sweaty.

Emma lifted up Hudson's travel basket and the man nodded and smiled. "Lovely ginger cat, bet it's his first time at sea, eh?"

Hudson yowled at him. He never spoke to any other human being other than Emma, so when he wanted to show he was either happy or sad he'd either purr or yowl.

Hudson's yowl always got people's attention. It was a yowl that was almost a roar...

Eeeeoooooowwwwlllll

(Which is probably why people use the word 'yowl.')

The man in the orange vest looked surprised. He leant down and examined Hudson, who sat still and stared back at him, his mouth firmly closed.

Emma understood, without Hudson even saying anything to her. He didn't want her to tell the man that Hudson had, indeed, already been to sea, and might even have been born on the ocean. And that he wanted, one day, to be a captain of his very own ship.

The man chuckled and waved Emma toward a short queue near the front of the ship where people with various baskets and dogs on leads, were waiting their turn to get onboard.

"Join that line," the man said.

"In Britain, we call it a 'queue'," Emma explained politely.

"Oh really? Well then join that *queue*," the man said looking a little annoyed.

> **Britishism: *Queue* – a line you wait in**

Emma decided she didn't like him, but she was so excited at being so close to boarding the ship that she immediately forgot him and walked quickly to stand behind a tall man in a long coat and an old fashioned hat.

At his feet sat a cute looking hairy little dog. It was shaggy and white, and it shivered slightly in the cool sea air.

Hudson stared down at it quizzically. Emma tried to move forward a little to see what the tall man looked like. In her mind she imagined that he had a thin face and big, pointy nose.

Suddenly, he turned around and she was right! He *did* have a thin face and a very, very pointy nose. Aon on his nose he wore a pair of round glasses behind which were small, green eyes.

At the same moment, his dog turned to look at Emma and Hudson and the rest of the family. He had a terrier's face that was bright and eager, and he looked as excited to be getting on the cruise ship as Hudson was.

"I hope that dog doesn't want to chase Hudson!" Little Brother smirked, almost as if he really hoped that the little dog *would* want to chase Hudson, but the dog looked very calm and kind and just kept panting eagerly.

"Hello, and who is this?" the pointy-nosed man asked. He had an American accent and he sounded like someone from one of the old films that Mum and Dad loved to watch on Sunday afternoons. The black and white ones that didn't seem to have much action in them, and there was always a lot of talking.

"This is my cat Hudson," Emma said. Then she looked at the man's dog; "And who is this?" Emma tried to say it in the same way that the pointy-nosed man had, but she couldn't quite do an American accent.

"Why, little lady, this is Tadeusz."

Emma frowned. She'd never heard that name before. She couldn't imagine how it was spelt, let alone what it meant. It sounded like tad-chew-ush.

The man could see that she was confused. He smiled a gentle smile and said, "We call him Tad. He's a Polish terrier."

Emma stroked Tad's head and Tad panted gratefully and stood up on his hind legs and pawed her coat. Hudson sat and watched with a curious look on his face. Tad turned his head to Hudson, and Emma worried that Hudson might yowl again or even hiss at Tad.

But he didn't.

Instead he just looked at Tad calmly. That was very unusual. Hudson was never, *ever* nice to dogs. Not to the dogs that lived near Emma and her family anyway. Hudson thought dogs were just... well... plain stupid. Emma tried to tell him that she had known some quite intelligent dogs - but Hudson would never listen.

Before they knew it, the queue began to move quickly as the passengers and their animals were checked and then allowed to go on board.

And there were so many different kinds of animals! Emma was amazed.

There were dogs – a lot of dogs. More dogs than cats. Hudson didn't seem to mind.

There were rabbits.

There were parrots and budgies, and one white dove.

There was a snake. Emma shivered. She really hoped it wouldn't escape. A snake on a ship!!! No!!

There were three hamsters and one gerbil.

Finally, Tad, the Polish terrier, was checked and issued with a tag that was attached to his collar.

"See you around," called the tall American man with the pointy nose.

"See you around," said Emma.

Then Hudson had to be checked. They stepped up to a long table where a lady in a white uniform sat. She had a lot of papers in front of her – lists and documents of all kinds – and a stapler and a stamp. She tickled the top of Hudson's head and declared, "Such an intelligent looking cat." Then she stamped his cat passport. (Cats *can* have passports, by the way).

Hudson purred, but Emma knew he was just being polite. He didn't need compliments. He *knew* he was intelligent, but not in a big-headed way.

"He is," Emma replied proudly. She loved it when people said nice things about Hudson. "He is a *very* clever cat," she said with a broad smile.

The lady put a cat-sized tag on Hudson's collar and tickled his head again, and Hudson purred again. This time he wasn't just being polite. He was starting to understand that this ship, and the people on it, were special.

Then, at long last, they were on the ship.

And what a ship it was!

6.

As Emma climbed up and up the stairs from the deck where she and Hudson had boarded, she wondered what she would see.

The last time she was on a cruise ship she remembered a really big space where there was a fountain and a big sparkling staircase and huge glittery lights that made everything shine.

It was becoming obvious that this ship – the *Magical Seas* – was different.

So different that Emma felt like the breath had been sucked out of her as she stepped down from the staircase and into an amazingly big and wide and very round area. It looked a bit like a spacecraft, a lot like a palace, and a little like a dream.

It was white. And red. *And* gold.

It was so tall that it went all the way up to the top of the ship where there was a round glass roof that let you see the bright blue sky.

A swirling fairy tale staircase curled around a glass lift that rose up and down with excited people staring out at the ship and all the buzzing activity on each deck.

Britishism: *Lift* – 'elevator.'

Emma's heart missed a beat. She caught her breath and wondered if any of this was real. Sometimes that happens; something you want so much comes true and you don't believe it's actually happening. It feels like a dream, and that can make you sad, because if it *is* a dream then you'll wake up and that magical thing you love so much isn't real.

Even if this *was* a dream, Emma decided to enjoy it while it lasted. So she kept moving round and round trying to see every detail of the ship all at once. Then she felt Hudson shifting in his basket, and she heard a plaintive yowl.

That yowl is too real to be in a dream!

At that moment, a hand was placed on her shoulder.

"It's wonderful, isn't it?" a soft voice said behind her.

Emma stopped turning. For a moment she felt dizzy, so she closed her eyes. Then she wondered if, when she opened them, she'd find that it all *had* been a dream. She really hoped that it hadn't.

"Don't worry, it's all real," the voice assured her. It was as if he'd read her mind.

Emma opened her eyes to see a man wearing a crisp white merchant marine officer's uniform and hat looking down at her.

"I think your cat needs to be taken to his quarters, don't you agree?"

Emma was amazed by how white the officer's uniform was. It was dazzling, perfectly crisp and stunningly clean.

"Reply to the officer," Mum said from behind Emma.

She realised that Mum, Dad and Little Brother were standing behind her. It was as if she'd completely forgotten that they were on board too!

The magical feeling of being on the ship had made her believe that only she, only Emma, only Emma and Hudson, were going on this adventure.

"Yes, Hudson needs to see his…" Emma was going to say 'cabin' but stopped herself.

"Cabin?" the officer suggested.

That's when Emma noticed that he had a name badge. She looked at it and realised that the officer had a name as well as a rank. *Chief Pet Officer: Perry Petty.* She laughed.

"Don't be rude, Emma!" Mum said sounding annoyed.

"No, don't worry. That's the reaction I usually get when people see what my name is," Perry said.

Mum squinted at his name badge, and she couldn't help chuckling.

"See!" Perry laughed. "Now, I can direct you to your cabin umm..." he hesitated in a way that would encourage Emma to tell him what her name was.

"My name is Emma, and this is Hudson." She lifted Hudson up to show him.

"Well, Emma and Hudson, let's show you to the Pet Deck. The world's one and only Pet Deck. Other ships might have kennels, but *this* ship has a Pet Deck that's been specially and carefully designed to give our passengers' pets the best voyage possible!"

Emma followed Chief Pet Officer Perry with a spring in her step.

This was going to be the best, most amazing, most enjoyable and most stupendous voyage ever!

*Definitely the best **EVER!***

7.

They stepped into the glass lift and the floor glowed gold as the heavy doors began to close with what sounded like a soft sigh. Emma felt a tingle on the back of her neck as if someone had whispered in her ear. Officer Petty quickly held the door to let the tall pointy-nosed American man in with Tad following obediently behind.

"Hello again," the man said. He saluted Officer Petty who returned the salute and then held out his hand to Emma. "I think it's time for a proper introduction; my name is Morgan Astor Hubbard the Third, and you are?"

"Emma…" she tried to remember her middle name so she could match his very long and impressive name, but her mind froze, and she forgot it. Sometimes that happens. You just forget something you have always known.

Morgan Hubbard Astor the Third didn't seem to mind that Emma had a very simple – and very short – name. He laughed and said "Emma! I had a Great Aunt called Emma and she was a very impressive lady. Emma Astor Morgan Hubbard Baines.

Hudson looked up at Emma as if to say, "You can't compete, so just stick to one name. It's enough. It's all you need to be you."

Yes - Emma could read Hudson's mind just by looking at how his ears twitched and how his mouth curled and the way his eyes flicked from her to Morgan Astor Hubbard the Third.

"Ah, Chief Pet Officer Petty, it's wonderful to meet you again," Morgan Astor…

(Let's just agree to call this pointy nosed but clearly very nice American gentleman by his first name, OK?)

Morgan ruffled Tad's head and said, "Now, Tad you treat this expert young man right. You do what he says, and you be good up there on the Pet Deck, you hear me Tadeusz Astor Hubbard!?"

Surely that poor dog doesn't have to put up with all those names!

Emma felt sorry for Tad, but it was obvious that he didn't seem to mind having so many names. Tad raised his paw and Morgan shook it like he was shaking a person's hand.

Then Tad looked at Emma and she could see that he was laughing inside. His owner was, to be honest, slightly over-the-top.

The lift doors sighed closed at last, and it began to rise gently upwards. Emma turned to watch the different decks of the ship go by. Through the glass she could see a library, quite a few bars, some plush lounges, a library, a big games room, the Kids Zone, and enormous restaurants as well as small ones.

One place caught Emma's eye: Cookie Heaven.

Emma LOVED cookies. All kinds of cookies. Big cookies and little cookies. Cookies with chocolate bits and cookies without chocolate bits. Chewy, crunchy cookies. Round and square cookies. Double-decker cookies. Any cookie was a great cookie!

She promised herself to go and visit Cookie Heaven just as soon as she'd seen Hudson safely to his place on the Pet Deck.

The lift seemed to sigh again as it slowed down and gently stopped at Deck 15.

This deck was different from the others. You couldn't see down to the other decks. The door opened out to a small landing in front of big wooden doors.

Chief Pet Officer Petty waved a small plastic card at a glowing disc on the wall next to the doors and they both swung open silently.

Emma followed Perry and Morgan into what was the most luxurious kennels, or cattery, or any kind of animal enclosure she'd ever seen.

Hudson sat up straight and licked his lips as if he'd just seen a huge bowl of Temptys.

In fact, there WAS a huge bowl of Temptys right in the middle of the deck. Just behind it was another bowl with some dog biscuits.

Tad barked, jumped up and pawed Morgan's leg.

"Be patient, Tad old chap, you'll soon be sick of them. I ordered you unlimited Taddies."

But Tad didn't really care about what might happen in the future, he just wanted the dog biscuits now.

"Taddies?" Emma heard herself saying. She didn't really believe that that's what the snacks were called.

"Oh, my dear," Morgan said, looking down at her with his soft, kind eyes, "My family owns the company that makes them, and they were called Taddies after our very special little friend here, Tad."

Emma looked at Tad. Hudson looked at Tad. Tad looked a little embarrassed in a way that only a Polish terrier could look embarrassed. His face seemed to say, "sure my owner is fabulously rich, but those treats are soooooo so good, I don't care what they're called."

"So, shall I show Hudson to his quarters?" Perry asked as he turned to Morgan. "Tad, of course, has his usual kennel. It's all ready, just the way he likes it."

Morgan saluted again and turned, pulling Tad away from the Taddies and walked away to the other side of the deck.

"Tad's cabin has been made to look and feel just like the kennel he has at home. We call them 'cabins' but they're not really cabins," Perry explained, walking to a row of big cages. Emma followed, Hudson looked eagerly out of his basket at the 'cabins' and the animals inside them.

Each cabin had a porthole – a small round window – and you could see the wide blue sea through it.

Emma had almost forgotten that they were on board a ship! Ever since she had got into the lift she felt like she was a in a palace, or a very plush hotel, or... well, not on a ship floating by a dock at a port.

The sight of the sea through the porthole reminded her that she was indeed on a very big, very grand ship. "Oh look, Hudson, you can see the sea whenever you want to!" she said.

Hudson purred happily.

That's because his cabin had soft cushions, a scratching pole with a little model of the ship's funnel on top of it, and small toys that looked like fish and mice. His bed was a big soft red and white striped basket. It looked really comfy.

"Now, if we hit some rough seas, well, then we have ways to keep our animals comfortable," Perry said in a reassuring tone.

"Oh Hudson won't get seasick," Emma said quickly, "He's used to the sea, that's where I found him and one day he wants to be master of his own ship!" Emma stopped herself. She put her hand to her mouth. What had she done!?

Hudson looked up at her with surprised eyes. The surprise started to turn to hurt. Emma had revealed his secret!

For a moment they all stood there, not saying anything. It was a completely awkward silence.

But Perry just nodded and smiled and stroked Hudson's head and finally he said – well, almost purred; "Hudson is a very, very special cat; that much we know already."

Hudson was reassured. He jumped from Emma's basket, landed softly on the cabin floor and started to roam around his living quarters for the next week. He liked it. He *really* liked it. Emma could tell. Hudson stood up on hind legs and peered out of the porthole.

At that moment, the ship's horn blew.

A deep, loud, rumbling sound that bounced around the deck and made the hairs on Emma's neck stand up and she felt a tingle run from the top of her head down her back to the tips of her toes.

Something very special was going to happen here. She could tell. Something special and something that would change her life and Hudson's life.

Something that would make their dreams come true.

Something *magical.*

8.

Once the ship's horn had blown, something louder echoed around the Pet Deck.

A dog's bark.

The loudest bark you ever heard!

A bark that could be heard around the world.

A bark that was bigger than any bite

The ship is shaking

Emma's bones are vibrating

The deck is rumbling

Hudson's fur is rippling

"Oh, he promised not to do that!" Perry cried and he rushed away, across the deck to a small cage on the opposite side to where Hudson would be staying.

It was the canine quarters, where all the dogs were staying. Emma was curious and she started to follow Perry. Hudson yowled, he wanted to come too.

"Are you sure? That bark must have come from a really huge hound. So huge that, if I were you,

I'd be frightened that it'll sniff you out and try to attack you," Emma said.

Hudson looked at her, a little disappointed.

"I'm not afraid of anything, especially some stupid dog, big or small," Hudson declared.

Emma picked him up and carried him in her arms to where Perry was shushing the barking hound through the bars of his cage.

Only...

Wait a minute...

Where's the dog?

There doesn't seem to be a dog in there...

Emma's mind raced through the possibilities: perhaps the dog was sick and was lying down behind his basket. Perhaps the dog was so big it made the cage dark because no light could get in through the little porthole...

I don't believe it!

She stared and stared. Perry held the smallest, cutest little Chihuahua you ever saw.

"His bark is bigger than... *HE* is!" Emma was stunned by what she saw.

Perry laughed. "That's very well put, Emma." He held up the little dog and Emma was sure she saw it smile.

A dog that can smile?!

(Dogs DO smile, you know)

But this dog smile is halfway between a smile and a growl

The little dog panted and squirmed when it saw Hudson, but it wasn't because he wanted to chase him. It looked like it wanted to say hello.

"This is Tarquin. We call him Big Tiny. Big Tiny, say hello to your new friends, Emma and Hudson."

Big Tiny opened his mouth and began to take a big breath...

Oh no!

He's going to bark!

"Remember what we said, Tarquin, no barking unless the ship's big horn is broken, ok?" Perry said.

Tarquin thought about that for a second, then flicked his tongue around his mouth and panted. His big eyes were wide with interest, as if he were excited to meet his new friends.

"His bark is bigger than... HE is!"

Hudson purred, lifted his left paw and waved. Tarquin did the same.

"See! They're already friends," Perry grinned. He put Tarquin back into his cage and closed the door. "OK, I think it's time for you to let Hudson settle in, Emma, why don't you join your family and explore the ship? I think you'll find that it's truly spectacular."

Emma really did want to explore the ship. She nuzzled Hudson and whispered, "I'll be back to see you before dinner, but I really want to see the ship and…"

"Go to Cookie Heaven," Hudson whispered. He knew Emma so well that he understood that she was aching to check out the cookies.

Emma laughed out loud as she walked quickly back to the other side of the deck. She put Hudson into his cabin and closed the door. She waved at him.

Then she suddenly felt sad.

She didn't really want to leave him.

"I'll be fine… as long as Tarquin doesn't bark again," Hudson reassured her.

Emma hesitated for a moment; she could hear the cookies calling her! She decided that Hudson would be fine and waved at him as she ran toward the lifts.

Hudson watched her. He loved Emma but he knew that something would change now that he was on this magical ship; that, at last, he would be able to do what he always wanted to do.

Go to sea.

Be a captain of his own ship.

And perhaps one day, maybe a long time in the future, find his mother... and his family.

He could feel that, at last, he was close to another world. Another very, very special world.

9.

Cookie Heaven turned out to be exactly what the name suggested it would be.

Heaven... with cookies

All kinds of cookies...

Big and small and all sizes in between

Any flavour you can think of

And all the flavours you never imagined could be flavours

Emma stared wide-eyed at the cookie menu. She'd never seen such a variety of flavours! So many combinations and possibilities! It was like a dream. A sugar-rush dream that felt both dangerous and delightful. Even impossible.

But it was possible

Because it was here

It was real...

And Emma couldn't decide what to have

Emma's mind went blank. Usually, she could see the image of the cookie she wanted in her mind, but here, now, on this ship, all she could see was a jumble of words and spinning pictures of cookies that wouldn't stay still enough to see what they were.

Then, out of nowhere, she heard a woman's voice say, "It's difficult to choose, isn't it?" The voice seemed to be above her. No, no maybe it was next to her. They floated in space for a moment and then, like chocolate chips coming together in the perfect cookie, they made a sentence that Emma could understand. She turned to see another crisp white uniform.

Cookie Heaven turned out to be amazing!

"I like the ginger cookies with white chocolate. They're my favourite," the woman sounded pleasant and very definite. She clearly knew what kind of cookies she liked the best.

For a moment, Emma couldn't match the voice to the person standing next to her looking up at the cookie menu. She was wearing a white uniform like Chief Pet Officer Petty wore, but her badges were different. On her shoulders were epaulettes – they're black with gold markings – Emma remembered a video she'd seen on YouTube about what they meant.

They had four gold bars with a square resting at an angle on the top of them.

It's the ship's captain!

She looks so nice...

Not just nice... but... clever

The kind of captain you want to sail a huge cruise ship like this one!

Emma wanted to make sure she didn't blurt out anything stupid, so she took a deep breath and said calmly, "I like the look of the cookie with Hundreds and Thousands.'"

Another voice came from behind Emma and the Captain, "Those aren't Hundreds and Thousands, they're Sprinkles." The voice was American and Emma recognised it straight away.

She turned to see Morgan rubbing his pointy chin with his long bony fingers as he looked up at the menu. Emma had just noticed that his chin was almost as pointy as his nose.

"What you just used, my dear Emma, is what I call a 'Britishism'"

"But Hundreds-and-Thousands isn't a word they're a *thing*. Well, a food actually. Well, a kind of decoration... a *sweet* decoration for... cakes and cookies."

"They're the same thing. In America we call them Sprinkles," Morgan said.

"Like you say candy and we say sweets," Emma asked.

"Exactly. A Britishism," Morgan replied, looking pleased with himself.

Britishism: *Sweets* – all kinds of candy but not chocolates

The Captain laughed and looked at Emma and said, "It's amazing how many Britishisms there are, and it's a lot of fun finding them."

"It's like we say 'line' for your 'queue,' Morgan added. "There are so many more, but, for now, let us contemplate all these scrumptious cookies."

"We say 'biscuits' for most of the things you call 'cookies'," Emma added.

"Yeah, but what we have here *are* actual cookies and, whatever you want to call them, and you can call them anything you want to, they look *soooo* delicious!," Morgan said. Then he looked back to the cookie menu, his eyes scanning all the different kinds and his pointy nose twitching as all the rich smells wafted around him.

"You're right, *these* are definitely just cookies," Emma said running her finger down the choices.

"Yes, yes, we don't have to be so precise." Morgan sounded a little annoyed now. The Captain winked at Emma and went back to debating which cookie to choose.

For a moment, they all stood there staring and trying to make an almost impossible decision. Which cookie to have?

Would it be...

Good Old Fashioned Plain Cookie?

Chocolate Chip cookie?

Choc Chip and Almond?

Cinnamon and Hazelnut?

Double Choc with Pistachio?

Pistachio Delight?

Macaroon Mystery?

Oatmeal Raisin?

Unraisinably Chocolatey?

"I like the sound of '*Unraisinably Chocolatey*,'" Morgan decided, "What do you think Captain?"

The Captain rubbed her chin as if to make a point to Morgan and finally answered, "I'll stick with Smarties. We call them Smarties in the UK and that's what we'll call them on this ship while I'm in charge."

"That's fair," Morgan said. Then he looked down at Emma, "And what would this young lady like?"

Emma hadn't actually made up her mind, but her mouth opened, and words came out before she even knew what she wanted to say, "I'll have what *she's* having."

"Let me," Morgan went to the counter and ordered the three cookies.

While he was getting the cookies, the Captain held out her hand and said, "I'm very pleased to meet you..." She paused to let Emma tell her what her name was, but Emma just stared at the gold buttons on her uniform and the name badge on her chest: *Captain Karina Martin.*

Suddenly, Emma's brain clicked back into action, and she shook Captain Karina's hand saying, "My name's Emma and I'm here with my family and my cat."

"Oh, that's wonderful! And your cat is already up on the Pet Deck no doubt?"

"Yes, and he loves it. His name is Hudson, and he loves the sea..." Emma wanted to tell Captain Karina the whole story all at once, but she knew it wouldn't make sense just to blurt it out. So instead she took a deep breath and smiled sweetly up at her.

Morgan returned with the cookies; each one carefully placed in their own brown paper bag. He handed one to Emma and then one to Captain Karina.

"I wish I could stay and chat, but I'll take my cookie to the bridge and munch on it as we sail into the open ocean. It's almost time." Captain Karina smiled at Emma and then winked at Morgan and turned, taking a little bite from her cookie, and left.

Emma watched her walk away. Captain Karina waved at passengers as they saw her and excitedly said 'hello' and she even stopped to pose for a photo with an old couple.

Morgan had begun nibbling his cookie. He looked like a bird pecking at a piece of bread. No. he actually looked like a squirrel nipping at a nut while looking nervously around for predators. It was as if he thought eating a cookie was not the kind of thing a man with so many names should do in public, but the cookies were so good that he couldn't help himself.

"Why do they call the place where the captain steers the ship the bridge?" Emma asked.

Morgan patted his lip with a fine handkerchief that he took from the top pocket of his jacket and began, "Long ago, when steamships used to go back and forth across the oceans, they had big paddles on either side. The captain and his crew steered the ship on a platform connected to both of them. It was a 'bridge' between them. That's why."

"Oh, I see," Emma said, but she wasn't really listening. She was thinking about how she might get Hudson onto the bridge so he could watch how Captain Karina commanded the ship. There he could learn what it takes to be a captain.

10.

Hudson felt the ship shudder and then his paws felt funny. They tingled and his whiskers twitched. The ship was moving sideways, away from the dock, and Hudson could feel the ship floating free from the ropes that he'd seen wrapped tightly around what looked like small post boxes on the pier.

> **Britishism:** *Post Box* – red boxes (usually on street corners) where British people place letters to be collected by the post-person. *Mail Box* in the US.

For a moment – just a very short moment – the feeling of being on the water made him feel odd for a moment. But then he remembered how much he liked being at sea. After all, he'd been born at sea. He knew that much. He couldn't remember where or how, of course none of us do, but his instinct told him that he was closer to home, wherever that was.

Closer to my family

Closer to my mother

Closer to... where I was born to be

The Pet Deck went quiet – totally silent – for a moment. All the animals were taking time to try and understand what had changed. Some of them didn't know they were even on a ship, and they couldn't understand the vibrations that were flowing through the deck beneath their feet.

Then a parrot squawked, and a pair of white doves began to flap their wings and made a weird noise that sounded like a... like a what?

A kazoo?

A strange musical humming sound that, after a few moments, became quite soothing. In fact, Hudson quite liked it.

Pssssst

Hudson jumped up to look out of his porthole. He could see the wide, flat waters of Southampton. They were grey like the clouds in the sky, and in the distance he could see rows and rows of cars. Southampton was one of the places where cars were imported into Britain from far, far away.

Psssst!

The ship began to turn, very slowly, but Hudson could feel the ship's engines far below. Right at the bottom of the ship, in the engine room, working hard to power the huge ship out into open waters.

Psssst!

Hudson's ear pricked up and twirled one way and then the other to work out where the strange hissing sound was coming from.

Was it a balloon deflating?

Pssssst!

Perhaps it was the air-conditioning or... NO! It couldn't be! An escaped snake!?

Hudson had never seen a snake – only on TV – but he knew deep down that he didn't like them. Not one bit.

He leaped up onto a shelf that was above his bed and carefully inspected the floor of his cabin. His quick eyes flicked from place to place trying to find a slithery slimy long snake!

Pssssst!

There it was again, but it wasn't coming from inside his cabin. It was coming from *outside.*

Hudson was sure that they didn't allow snakes on a ship. Even a ship that allowed all kinds of pets. Snakes would be the limit. No one wanted a snake on a ship!

He hopped down and went to the edge of the cabin and peered outside. Across the deck he could see Tad, his tongue hanging out and looking eager. He was wagging his tail so fast it could have been a propeller.

"At last!" said Tad.

"Why didn't you just call me?" Hudson asked.

"I didn't want to attract attention," Tad explained in a clear voice. He had an American accent, like his owner, Morgan Astor Hubbard the Third.

"But you just did," Hudson pointed out, pointedly.

"I had to… or you wouldn't have heard me."

"So, why try NOT to attract attention, when you wanted my attention?" Hudson tried hard not to sound annoyed. He was a little. But not too much.

"I only wanted YOUR attention."

"Well, now you've got it, what do you want?" Hudson was teasing Tad. He liked the look of the Polish terrier. He was friendly, and, for a dog, seemed quite clever.

"So, I was wondering… I mean… you're, like, ready for… you know…"

Hudson frowned. The dog might be quite clever, but he wasn't making any sense. "Ready for - what?"

"I mean, it's why most of us are here right?"

"Why are most of us here? For what?" Hudson was little confused.

"You really don't know!!?" Tad looked surprised. He took a deep breath and was about to say something – something that would explain what he really meant – when he stopped.

Someone had come onto the Pet Deck. They heard some footsteps first, then a deep voice humming something – a little musical riff. Humming a strange little tune. Not just humming but adding a beat to it too.

Badum... badum... sssst... badum badumm... hey hey hey

The humming had a nice rhythm to it, and it was perfectly in tune.

Then a man who looked as if he was made of rubber wearing a very blue and very shiny suit appeared between Hudson and Tad's cabins. His body looked like it was pulsing to a hidden rhythm. He walked so lightly and moved with such easy grace it was like he was always just about to dance. His polished black shoes glinted in the lights.

"Hey, hey, Kat my man! KAT you ok?"

Tad and Hudson both watched as the man stood by a cage just a little way up from theirs. They saw a glistening snout appear at the bars along with two bright little eyes. A long and lean brown animal then stretched up and placed its small paws on the bars, it's nose sniffing the air and its mobile tongue licking its lips.

"The world's coolest kat!" The man said.

Whatever that creature is, it's not a cat! Hudson thought.

The coolest Kat!

The creature began to tap its claws on the bars. And, after a moment, Hudson started to tap his front paw. That surprised him. This creature – this not a cat creature – *did* have a sense of rhythm.

Hudson could see that Tad was also nodding along to the beat. The man in the very blue suit began to hum a tune and then pretend that he was playing a trumpet.

The other animals: cats, dogs, birds, rabbits, gerbils (but no snakes) came to the bars of their cages and listened too.

When the music stopped there was a round of barks and meows, squawks and trills, and a general wagging of tails and a fluttering of wings.

"You learned good, Kat, you're the one and only mongoose that's got the music in ya soul! Duke Spellington is proud of you, you cool, cool Kat!!"

Mongoose!

That's what that is?

A mongoose.

A mongoose! On a ship!

Who has a mongoose for a pet?!

And then calls it a cat?

But the way he says it sounds more like…

That's it! KAT.

With a K.

71

Hudson realised that if anyone was going to have a mongoose – a musical mongoose at that – for a pet, it would be a jazz musician on a cruise ship. He didn't know why, but it suddenly made sense. Sometimes that happens; even the strangest things make sense when you see them in real life.

So, really, this all made sense.

"Pssst!"

"Psssssst!"

"You don't have to keep doing that, Tad," Hudson said.

"It makes sense, that's why the mongoose is here and it's why I'm here and it's why YOU'RE here," Tad whispered panting in between most of his words. He was excited and nervous at the same time.

"I really don't know what you're talking about," Hudson said. But, deep down, he could really feel that something strange was going to happen. The feeling had been growing with every hour that passed. In fact, it had been growing ever since he first heard about this cruise.

He knew, deep down, that his life would change in strange and exciting ways. He didn't quite know how, but he was excited to find out. His instincts told him that the sea was a place where dreams come true.

11.

Emma read through the ship's Daily Schedule. That's a list of all the events that are happening on the ship, from trivia competitions to painting classes, films and shows, competitions on the pool deck, and even lectures. It also listed what was going on in the Kids' Club, which was on Deck 10 near the back of the ship. The aft. That's what they call the back of a ship. It's also called the stern. Emma learned that the first time she was on a cruise.

She had been to Kids' Clubs before, but she wasn't so keen this time. She thought that she was now a little too old. She wasn't, but she just *felt* too old.

"You should go," Mum said gently.

"Go, you'll meet new friends," Dad agreed.

"Don't go, you're embarrassing," Little Brother groaned.

Emma promised to go – soon. She wanted to explore the ship on her own first.

What Emma really loved about being on a cruise ship was that she could do a lot of things on her own. She didn't have to follow Mum and Dad around all the time, and now that she was old enough to explore without the possibility of getting lost. Not too lost anyway. And the ship's crew were always around to help her if she did.

"I might just go to a lecture," Emma said.

Mum, Dad and Little Brother looked at her in shock.

"A lecture?" Mum was surprised.

"What kind of lecture?" Dad asked.

"Booooring!" Little Brother groaned. He could never just say something, he had to make the words sound like a groan.

Emma ignored him. "It's called 'The True Magic of the Sea'" she said pointing to the listing in the Daily Schedule.

"Sounds nice," Mum said.

"Magic? What's magic about the sea? It's just the... sea," Dad said.

"Booooooorring!" Little Brother groaned.

"I don't know what it *means*, I just think it sounds... cool." Emma stood up determined to go.

"Maybe it will be cool," Mum said.

"What's cool about the sea?" Dad said.

"B'b'b'b'b *BOOOOORING!*" Little Brother screamed.

Mum and Dad frowned at him. Really they should have told him off. They never did, which is why he groaned so much.

Emma stood up and looked at her watch. She had an old-fashioned watch with hands and numbers and a little wheel you turned to wind it up, and it ticked. "I don't want to miss it."

"Go and get good and BOOOOORED!" Little Brother whispered though it still sounded like one of his groans.

He was soooo annoying. Emma ignored him and walked away trying to look as if she knew exactly where she was going.

They had been sitting in the buffet. Little Brother had eaten too much cake, and Dad had enjoyed a burger (with everything – too much! – on it). Mum had finished a plate of sushi, which she loved. and she'd almost screamed with joy when she first saw fresh sushi at one of the food stations.

They were happy. That was good. Emma knew she could leave them and do her own thing. Because *she* was the one who always wanted to go on a cruise, she felt almost responsible for her parents and her brother. She wanted them to enjoy their time on the ship. She would do anything to make sure that they had a great time. But she also wanted to enjoy the ship in her own way. And looking at the sea, walking around and exploring the ship, watching how the crew members worked, and seeing all the other passengers was a big part of what she loved about cruising.

Emma stood in the main atrium – the one with the great big glass lift – and looked at the map of the ship.

The lecture was going to be in a room called The Melville Lounge. In the Daily Schedule it said that it was on Deck 4, Aft. That meant towards the back of the ship. On a ship that's called the aft, which is also known as the stern.

But which way was that?

Suddenly, she remembered something she'd seen on YouTube about how some cruise ships have secret signals woven into the carpets on the floors, or little signs in the decorations on the walls.

She looked down at her feet. She was standing on a rich carpet which had a wavy pattern in different shades of blue. She looked closer. The pattern was made of little dolphins. And whales. And swordfish. All kinds of fish. And mammals because, of course, Emma knew that whales and dolphins are actually mammals. And those fish and mammals were...

YES!

That's it!

*So simple... so **brilliant!***

The creatures were all going one way. So, their tails must be coming from the back. (The Aft or stern, remember?). She spun herself around on her heels to go in the right direction and bumped into a man carrying what looked like a black suitcase – or actually it was more of a box.

"Sorry!" she said.

"Did you just work out what the carpet means?" the man smiled and looked down at the carpet and then up at Emma with a knowing smile on his broad face.

Emma looked up and, for a moment, she was startled. He had a very kind face, but he also had a black eyepatch over his left eye. He reminded her a of a pirate she had seen in a film, but he didn't have a big moustache or a pirate's hat and he didn't carry a sword. So, of course, he wasn't *actually* a pirate. At least, he didn't look like one. Not really. He also carried a black box. Quite a big one. Might that be where he kept his treasure? Emma smiled at the thought.

"Where are you headed?" the man asked.

"To the lecture. The True Magic of the Sea," Emma replied a little nervously.

"Well, that's a coincidence, I'm headed that way too," he said with a kind smile. He had a musical voice. He wore a white suit, a light blue shirt and a red bowtie. His hands were long and graceful.

"Heck, that's where I'm headed. We'll go together!" He turned around and pointed in the right direction.

"It's in the Melville Lounge, Deck 4, aft," Emma said.

"That's precisely where it is. And it's in this direction. Follow me."

The man (who was definitely *not* a pirate) started walking and Emma couldn't help but check the carpet to see if he was really going the right way. And he was. He was going in the direction of the fishes' tails. He had a long stride, so she had to run to catch up with him.

"Have you been to a lecture on a ship before?" Emma asked the man breathlessly as she tried to keep up.

"Oh many times."

"Are they good?"

"That's a matter of opinion."

"Do you enjoy them?"

"Always."

"And what about this lecture?"

"You'll see."

Before Emma knew it, they had walked through a restaurant, an art gallery, and a bar. They arrived at a big round space that had chairs and tables where passengers could play board games and do puzzles.

An old couple were starting what looked like a very complicated puzzle – at least a thousand pieces! They looked up and seemed to be startled by the man in a white suit with an eye patch carrying a big black box.

"Good afternoon!" he said and then bowed. In an instant he'd slipped his fingers into the top pocket of the old man's jacket and, with a flourish and suddenly...

A bunch of paper flowers appeared!

Who is this guy!?

He looks like a pirate!

Is this a dream?

Emma couldn't believe what she'd just seen. The man – who Emma was now convinced was a magician – smiled broadly at the couple and their shock turned to laughter. They shook the man's hand and then he turned to Emma and said, "Let's go inside, or we'll be late."

She followed him through two big, heavy wooden doors and found herself in what resembled a small theatre with a stage at the far end. Emma looked up and saw that the ceiling had pinpoints of light sparking all across it. It reminded her of the night sky. As her eyes got used to the low lighting she realised that the ceiling was a big, rounded dome.

"You can sit there if you want to, you'll get the best view," the man said, pointing to a seat in the front row. There were already quite a few people in the room. They began to applaud, and Emma wondered why they were clapping her. She felt embarrassed. So she sat down and turned to the stage.

The man was now standing on it. His box had turned into a kind of table. A magician's table. He bowed and the audience clapped even harder.

THIS is the man who's going to give the lecture!

Emma's heart raced. She realised that the lecture was also – a MAGIC show!

12.

It was 'walkies' time. That's what Chief Pet Officer Perry Petty said when he appeared on the Pet Deck as the clock by the main door struck eight bells.

Eight bells?

What time is that?

It's actually 4 pm.

Hudson knew that because he knew almost everything about how ships work. It was the end of the 'afternoon watch.'

Perry opened Tad's cage and attached a lead to his collar. Then he walked along, opened Big Tiny's cage and was careful to put his finger to his lips to remind the little dog to stay quiet and not to bark. Big Tiny seemed to understand him, but Tad looked worried and stayed as far away from the little Chihuahua as he could. Which wasn't very far at all. Not far enough to protect his ears, anyway.

Hudson pressed his nose to the door of his cabin. He wanted to get out and see the sea from the Pet Promenade Deck. He yowled as sadly as he knew how. That made Perry turn to look at him. He thought for a second then stepped over to Hudson, the two dogs following behind him on their leads.

"Will you promise to stay on the deck and not skittle away to explore on your own, Hudson?" asked Perry.

Hudson turned as if to say, "Would I, a very intelligent cat, do anything as naughty as that?"

Perry understood instantly. Hudson wondered if he could actually *talk* to Perry, the way he did with Emma, but he decided not to try. He didn't want to talk to any other human but Emma. It wouldn't feel right. It was *their* secret. He wanted it to stay that way.

Perry unlocked the door to Hudson's cabin and picked him up with his free hand. "Come on, let's see how you do." He had a soft voice. The nicest human voice that Hudson had heard since he first met Emma on Brighton beach.

Out on deck, Hudson's nose twitched immediately. He closed his eyes as the sea breeze ruffled his fur and the bright sun began to warm his back.

Nothing else feels like the air at sea

Nothing else smells like the sea

Nothing else sounds like the sea

Nothing else makes you feel so free as the sea!

Perry put Hudson down on the deck. The railing had special webs of mesh between each post and steel bars to stop any animal falling through, either down to the next deck or into the sea.

Tad and Big Tiny started their walk. Tad wanted to talk to Hudson, but Perry pulled him by the lead to get him walking, so he could only say something each time he came around to where Hudson was sitting, watching the sea. He was happy doing just that. When Tad came round the first time, he said…

"My owner, Morgan, was telling this man with…"

And he passed, looking eager to keep talking. Tad strained a little on his lead, but Perry kept walking. Big Tiny's thin, little legs looked as if they were pumping really hard to keep up, but he was managing it. Tad said…

"…an eye-patch who does this really great magic and knows all about…"

He was gone again.

Hudson watched the seabirds riding the wind and following the ship. That meant they were still close to land. Tad appeared again…

"… how they were about to choose the new crew for their very special…"

Hudson looked down to see a small boat floating behind the ship. It was the Pilot, a special boat with a person who helps guide the huge cruise ship through the sea and make sure it stays in the parts of the port that were deep enough for it.

"...new cruise ship which is just for children and only exists..."

Hudson wondered what Emma was doing at that moment. Perhaps she was with Little Brother in the Kid's Club. Perhaps she was still at Cookie Heaven trying to choose between all the different but amazing cookies. That was more likely.

Tad's voice came around again...

"...in a very special world where the ship is crewed by animals and commanded by..."

Perry kept the dogs walking. Hudson always thought it was strange how dogs couldn't just exercise on their own. Why did they need humans to take them for walks? Cats don't need any human to take them for a walk because cats are cleverer than dogs. Although, Hudson didn't want to say that out loud, and he didn't have any actual evidence, but he suspected it was true.

"...a very special animal who knows the sea really, really well, and I really, really think that..."

Hudson watched as the Pilot boat slowed down and turned around to head back to shore. The men on board waved up at the bridge as it bobbed in the waves and motored away.

Now the *Magical Seas* was getting closer to the wide, wide and very deep ocean.

"...YOU are the one animal that they KNOW can command that ship and be its..."

Hudson was startled. What was Tad talking about? What ship run by animals? What special world in which only children can go on a cruise? What magician?

He turned and watched as Perry walked with the two dogs behind him at the far end of the Pet Promenade Deck. It was longer and wider than Hudson realised and, suddenly, they seemed to be taking a long, long time to get back to where he was standing.

At last, they approached...

"...I think that's going to be you!

You're going to be the captain... Captain Hudson!"

Hudson's ears pricked up. His whiskers perked up. His eyes lit up. He looked into the distance, his brain conjuring pictures of himself as... a captain.

Captain...

Hudson?

Captain?

Hudson?

Yes,

CAPTAIN HUDSON!

Yes. Yes, that sounded REALLY good.

Totally, totally perfect!

"I think that's going to be you!"

13.

The man in the white suit with the black eye-patch over his left eye stood on the stage and looked out across the audience.

Emma sat upright and watched intently; her eyes just couldn't help themselves; they were fixed on that almost blindingly white suit. As the lecture started, the already dim lights were turned off and a spotlight shone on the man. His white suit seemed to glow, and he looked bigger than he did before.

"Good afternoon, my name is Peter, and I want to tell you about the magic of the sea. It isn't just water... like the water in this cup..." He picked up a jug of water that was sitting on a small table with a black cloth over it. He held it up and turned from one side of the stage to the other to show it to the audience.

"Yes, it's – *water* - but..."

At that moment he jerked the jug upwards, and the water came out in a long splash that curved up into the air. Everyone in the front row, including Emma, raised their hands and cowered a little expecting to be splashed by the water. But then...

Then... THEN!

Peter waved his hands and, as if by magic...

And it WAS magic

The water curved back towards the stage and formed itself into a ball.

A ball of water!?

Everyone gasped in amazement. Emma had never seen a trick like it. Not even on TV, where it would probably have been a special effect anyway. But this was real. She could *see* it was totally real! She sat there, wide-eyed, her mouth open in amazement.

Holding the ball of water in his hands, Peter turned it around and around. It was spinning in his hands, floating in the air. The light from the spotlight made it shine with ever changing colours -

Blue, yellow, green, silver...

It sparkled, flowed and hovered and it was mesmerising.

"Over seventy percent of our planet is covered by the ocean. One, huge, deep, interconnected ocean. The seven seas are really ONE really enormous and continuous sea brimming with life and energy," he said as he continued to spin the ball of water. Now it looked like an entire planet made of water spinning in the immense blackness of the universe.

"It's the ocean that makes our world look like a polished marble when you see it from way up in space. That's what many of the very few people who have seen it from there say. What does it look like to you?"

Someone from the audience shouted out, 'A big drop of clear H-two-O – that's what water is!' The voice was a young one. It sounded like a boy.

Peter nodded, and replied, "Yes, H-two-O, you're right. That's the chemical name for water, and this is just a drop of the immense amount of water that's in the ocean. That's exactly right, well done."

Emma looked back to see where the voice had come from. She saw a boy of about her own age with black rimmed glasses on. He looked very pleased with himself, but also totally fascinated by what Peter was saying. She wondered if, like her, he was a kid who just loved being at sea.

"We think we know a lot about the oceans, but we don't really. It's the least explored habitat on Earth. Habitat means an environment in which plants and animals live. And the ocean has so many different species of plants and animals that it's impossible to count them all. We don't even know what they all are, and some of them we have never ever seen. All within this spinning ball of water!"

Emma wondered how Peter could keep that water spinning in the air. She'd never seen a magician do that before. It was incredible. She knew that when she told Mum and Dad and especially Little Brother about Peter and his magic they just wouldn't believe her.

"You can call Earth the Blue Planet, but water isn't blue. Water reflects or absorbs the colours in the light that hits it and passes through it, and it can be grey or green and a thousand shades of blue. But what's really important is that water is the substance that gives life to us all in one way or another. Which is why it's so precious."

Suddenly Peter clapped his hands and the water ball spun around and dropped back into the jug. Emma heard a plunking sound and saw a few drops of water splash onto Peter's suit. The audience clapped. Peter took a bow, and then said, "Now, ladies and gentlemen, boys and girls, you know that without the oceans there would be no life on earth. No you, no me, no pets and no… cookies, and no…"

He turned to look at Emma, "…especially, no *custard creams!*" Peter winked at her.

Emma froze.

How does he know that custard creams are my favourite British biscuit? (So much better than Oreos!)

Can he read my mind?!

"That's why water is magic. And it's why when you go to sea, your life always changes. You might not notice, but you're always different when you return home from a voyage."

Emma knew he was right.

I already feel really, really different!

The magic show ended, and everyone clapped and cheered. Emma slipped out of the theatre and went as quickly as she could to see Hudson.

14.

"Hudson, Hudson, you'll never guess what I just saw!" Emma said breathlessly as she ran toward Hudson's cabin on the Pet Deck.

But he wasn't there.

The cage was empty. So was Tad's, and Big Tiny's too. In fact, most of the cages where dogs were being kept were empty.

They all must be on the Pet Promenade Deck getting some fresh air and exercise

Emma looked for the door that led to the outside when she heard a voice behind her.

"They went walkies, walkies, walkies!" It was a squeaky, excited little voice. Suddenly Emma heard a metallic bang. Right next to a little animal appeared clinging to a wire mesh cage just over her head.

"You gave me a fright!" Emma said. She blinked and rubbed her eyes because what she saw looked like an agile little monkey.

"They go walkies walkies, walkies... unfair, unfair!" The monkey sounded sad.

"Did you want to go walkies?" Emma asked. She was not surprised by talking animals anymore. Until she came on this voyage she thought that Hudson was the only talking animal in the world, but now she knew she was wrong. The world was FULL of talking animals as long as you knew how to listen.

"Jumpies, jumpies, jumpies!" the monkey said gleefully.

Emma thought she knew what kind of monkey she was, but she didn't want to hurt her feelings just in case she was wrong. So she said, "Can I ask? Are you a... a lemur?"

"Bingo!" the lemur said, its black and white striped tail wagging left to right and up and down in excitement.

"So, actually you're *not* a monkey. I learned that at school. Lemurs are primates," Emma sound proudly. "We are too," she added. "Humans, I mean."

The lemur looked at her quizzically. It clearly did not matter to Bingo that she was not a monkey or that humans were primates. "What's your name?" Emma asked.

"Bingo!"

"No... what's your name?"

"BINGO!" the lemur screamed. So, clearly, that was her name. Then she ran around her cage four times, jumping on and off what looked like a tiny swing.

Bingo Bingo Bingo!

"That's a very... energetic name," Emma said.

"Ginger cat is outside!" Bingo pointed to the door that led out to the Pet Promenade Deck. It was frosted, which was why Emma hadn't realised it led outside.

"Thank you, Bingo, you're a very special primate. I'd like to talk to you more, but I need to find my cat," Emma said, just turning to leave.

"We can ALL can talk!" Bingo shouted in her small, shrill voice. "All the animals can talk on this ship. That's why we're here."

Emma turned back and asked, "And why are you here, Bingo?" Emma was very curious now.

"This is where they get the animals for the other world," Bingo jumped around, left to right, up and down, round and round and then ended up swinging on the tiny swing-set.

Emma didn't ask what the 'other world' was. Not because she didn't want to know. She was so very, very curious, but because deep down she already knew what was going to happen. Something special and something sad too. Sad for her. But something she would have to accept because, well because life was like that.

"Could you keep quiet?" another voice murmured, this time from across the Pet Deck. Emma turned to look where the voice came from. It was a tired, almost grumpy voice, deep and halfway between a sentence and a purr.

Emma looked around to see a big black cat licking its paws and looking at her with big, yellow eyes which would seem annoyed if they didn't also look so sleepy.

"I'm sorry, I'm just going out," Emma said.

"Then GO out! And don't slam that door. People are always slamming that door!" the cat huffed. Emma could now see it was a very plump cat. More than plump, FAT.

A fat cat!

Hilarious.

"That was the wind," Emma said.

"Don't blame other people or things for your own mistakes," the cat mumbled.

"I wasn't blaming the wind... actually... it wasn't my mistake... actually..."

"Oh stop saying 'actually!' It's *actually* so annoying!" The cat laid back and let its four paws stick up in the air over its very round white tummy. A black cat with a white tummy. Emma thought he actually looked quite cute even though he was a very grumpy puss.

"You're the owner of that Hudson fella aren't you?" the plump cat said.

"I am... and you are?"

"Bingo!" screeched Bingo jumping up and down and bashing the mesh on his cage with both his feet and his hands.

The ample cat covered his ears and moaned. "I can't wait for the storm so we can get out of here. And that monkey is NOT coming with us!"

Emma was about to correct the cat and inform him that Bingo was in fact a primate when her brain focused on one of the words he had just said:

Storm?

Coming with us?

"Is there going to be a storm?" Emma asked.

"Bingo!! Bingo!!"

"It can't come quick enough. *SHE* isn't coming," he said waving a lazy paw at the Lemur, "and thank goodness. Too noisy for a cruise ship full of children." The substantial cat nestled into his basket and licked his paws again.

"What's your name?" Emma asked.

"Marmaduke. *Mister* Marmaduke Morple, CEO."

"C-E-O?" Emma had heard that word before – actually it's a set of letters that sounds like a word – and she thought she knew what it meant but she didn't want to guess because Marmaduke would probably think she was stupid.

"Is there going to be a storm!?"

"It's not a word it's an acronym; a C and an E and an O – Chief Executive Officer. It means I'm the boss," Marmaduke Morple proclaimed. He licked his lips again and then said, "We have come across the magic wave to get some crew, but I don't like being at sea, always get so seasick so have to take medicine and the medicine makes me so sleepy," Marmaduke yawned.

Then he started to purr in a way that suggested he was about to fall asleep. "Said enough, said enough... you talk too much Marmaduke Morple," he said sleepily. "Don't you ever learn? Do you never learn. You do your best thinking when you're sleeping. Sleep. *Sleep.* SLEEP!"

And suddenly he began to snore. In that very special, unique and sleepy way that cats snore. Only more so because he was such a big cat.

Storm?

Magic Wave?

Emma wanted to wake him up and ask some very important questions, but he was snoring, and his lips puckered and made a flapping sound after every third snore. Her mind was awash with questions. It was as if the storm was starting to brew and gather power in her brain.

At that moment, Hudson, Tad and Big Tiny came through the door from the Pet Promenade Deck, followed by Chief Pet Officer Perry Petty.

15.

Emma froze. She really wanted to know what Marmaduke was talking about, but she didn't want to reveal to Perry that she could talk to the animals.

"Emma! Are you having a great time on the ship?" asked Perry.

"I'm having a wonderfully interesting time," Emma replied as Perry led Big Tiny to his cage, picked him up and put him inside. Big Tiny opened his mouth wide, and everyone stared at him waiting to see if he would yawn or bark.

He yawned.

"The sea air does all the animals so much good," Perry explained, as he opened Tad's cage and ushered the Polish terrier inside. Emma thought she saw Tad glance at her with a knowing look. Hudson purred and rubbed himself against Emma's leg and then returned to his cabin.

There was something in the way Hudson looked up at Emma that told her that there was something brewing. Something that Hudson knew and understood. Something that, she could tell, he wanted. He wasn't afraid. He was eager. She felt better.

Sometimes it's best to just let life unfold, and Emma was realising that now. There was a reason they were on this cruise. A reason why Mum and Dad had booked it. Not one that they understood, but it was just meant to be. And when something is meant to be, it's probably best to just accept it and see what life brings you.

"I heard there might be a storm," Emma said.

Perry nodded as he checked on the other animals. He looked into Marmaduke's cage and chuckled, "This cat never does anything other than sleep," he said.

"He looks like a very... important cat," Emma said wondering if Perry might explain who he really was.

Perry looked at Emma. He was just a little surprised by what she'd said. "Yes, you could say that. He belongs to a very important gentleman."

"Oh, does he?" Emma said.

"The gentleman who owns... this ship. In fact, he owns the entire cruise line."

"Really!?"

"Yes, really, and he's on board with his grandson. A very interesting boy. He knows just about everything there is to know about cruise ships and ocean liners," Perry said.

At that moment, Emma remembered the boy who'd shouted out the chemical formula for water during the magic lecture.

I bet that's him!

I thought he was that kind of...

Nerd?

If HE'S a nerd, then I am too.

Nerd's the wrong word

Enthusiast. That's a better word.

"You two should get together and have a chat," Perry suggested with a smile. Then he thought for a moment, "And yes, there is the possibility of a storm. When you're at sea, there's always a chance of a storm, but storms are..." Perry smiled reassuringly, "These ships are built to sail through them. And some people really enjoy the experience. It's exciting."

The way he said 'exciting' made Emma feel better. She'd been on a ship in rough weather before, and she didn't get seasick – well, only a little – and so she wasn't worried. What she really wanted to ask about, but didn't dare to, was what Marmaduke meant when he said that the storm would be his chance to go back to his job as CEO... of what?

"You look very... curious," Perry said.

"Do I?" Emma replied.

"I don't mean - you are a curious thing - but you look like you really want to know more about something. Is there something you want to ask me about?" Perry had a friendly face and Emma knew that she could dare to ask him about what was about to happen. But she decided not to.

Let's let things happen

See what it all means

It's bound to be exciting

16.

Dad loved jazz. So Dad suggested they go to the Atlas Bar where a Jazz Quartet was going to play.

Mum hated jazz so she didn't want to go. Little Brother just wanted to stay in the Kid's Club. He said that jazz was 'pants!' and Mum told him to be polite, so he just kept shouting 'Pants!'

Britishism: ***Pants!*** **– something that's really bad as in boring or rubbish.**

Emma told Dad that she would go with him if she could have a fizzy drink.

Britishism: *fizzy drink* **–** *The* **US's soda.**

Then she changed her mind and said that she'd have some squash.

Britishism: *Squash:* **A flavoured powder or cordial you add to water to make a tasty drink**

Emma didn't really like Jazz, but she'd been hearing it since she was little, so she was used to it. Strangely, it helped her to think.

The Atlas Bar was high up on Deck 10 and at the front of the ship – the Bow. It had a long, curved set of large windows with chairs and tables arranged so passengers could sit and have a drink and watch the ship moving toward the wide, very straight horizon.

The bar curved right around the back of the large room, and there were five bar staff working behind it, serving drinks. Waiters walked around with a tray in one hand and a bunch of little white napkins in the other. They would ask people if they wanted a drink, take their order, and then put a napkin in front of each guest.

When a waiter approach their table, Dad asked for a beer and Emma ordered her squash. Blackberry flavour. Then she looked out to sea, and it looked different to how it had looked just an hour ago. It was darker and, strangely, the water seemed thicker.

"Bit of swell coming up," Dad muttered with a tinge of excitement in his voice.

Emma knew that when the waves in the sea changed from being small and light to being deeper and higher with little crests of foam playing across them, there was a storm brewing.

"Don't those breaking waves out there look like... little white horses in the distance," Dad said.

Emma grinned. She liked that simile. Not 'smiley' – that's how she used to say the word when she was a little younger and learned about the difference between a simile and a metaphor. Although, if she was honest, she didn't quite know the difference every time she heard one.

"White horses? That sounds nice,"

"They're running away from the storm," Dad continued, "They know what's coming"

"Do you think there's going to be a storm?"

"Probably. Mum will stay in bed. I hope they'll let me walk out on deck – but that can be dangerous because of the wind and doors slamming and so on. So, probably not. But you never know. I'll go when it's brewing and see how long before they tell me to come inside."

Emma didn't like the idea of Dad walking around in a storm. Also, she hoped she wouldn't get sick. She wanted to go and see Hudson when the storm started – *if* it came – so she'd be there when...

When what?

I don't know what

But I know it will be important

In the middle of the Atlas Bar was a round stage. It was only a small one, just six inches of raised wood painted black – but it had a grand piano on it and chairs with music-stands in front of them and a big double bass resting on a stand.

As the waiter put their drinks down on the table Emma looked away and Dad signed the bill. Then she heard the tinkle of piano keys. She turned back to the stage and there was a jazz band there. And the man at the piano was the man in the very, very blue suit.

"Hello, hello cool kats - Welcome to the *Magical Seas* and the Atlas Bar. This is where we live, and we sail, and we be cool, and we groove to the sounds of... *jaaaazz!*"

The band started to play a tune and Emma watched them. The music sounded so very different when it was being played right there in front of you – live! And Emma was fascinated by the man playing the piano. His eyes were closed, and he swayed in time with the double bass and the drums. Next to him a clarinet player also moved in time with the beat.

Dad turned from the sea and watched the band. He was totally into the music and the whole vibe of the bar. That made Emma feel good. And the music sounded good too. Maybe, just maybe she actually liked jazz.

At the end of the tune, the piano player nodded as the guests clapped.

"Thank you, thank you, y'all the coolest kats on this ship, that's fo'sure, and we are the Duke Spellington Quartet, and I, well I'm Duke Spellington, I ain't no good at spellin' but I'm ex-cell-lent at groovin' and me and the guys' only mission in life is to put you in tha groove! Tha groove for a smooth, smooth sailin' ex-per-riensssssss, even if the storms they come rattlin' along. OK?"

People clapped, someone shouted, "Cool" and the quartet started up again.

"Hello."

Emma heard a voice she recognised, but she didn't know where it had come from. She looked behind her, no-one. She looked to her left - no-one.

"Hello."

She looked to her right and there stood the boy with the glasses from the magic lecture.

17.

Hudson could feel the ship move a little more. His paws took a while to get used to the gentle rolling of the deck, but he didn't feel queasy. There was a very deep memory – deep, deep down in the darkest corners of his mind – of his mother whispering in his ear, "You were born with sea legs little Hudson. You were born in a storm, and you'll never be afraid of the wind or the rain or the seas no matter how rough they get."

Hudson's eyes stung for a moment. That moment when you feel you want to cry but you know you mustn't. The moment when you feel sad, but you're not really sad, when the memory that's making your eyes sting is actually a happy memory.

Now, Hudson wanted the storm to come. He wanted the next part of his life to start. It was time for him to move on. To fulfil what he believed was meant to be. His destiny. That's what humans called it – 'destiny.' Something you're meant to be, something you're born to do, a place where you must go to be happy and be the person you are.

Chief Pet Officer Perry came through the doors to the Pet Deck, and he was followed by a crew member from the catering department pushing a trolley with the animals' evening meals.

Tad wagged his tail excitedly and panted as he waited for his Taddies. Marmaduke opened one eye and groaned. This was the noisiest part of each day – feeding time. He edged himself to the front of his cabin and licked his lips. He wasn't too queasy to have a snack, clearly.

Bingo screeched, Kat the mongoose tapped out a rhythm that Hudson recognised. It was from a tune that Emma's dad liked to listen to on his old fashioned stereo music player at home.

Perry opened Hudson's door and put a bowl of water and a bowl of Temptys next to it. He looked at Hudson with a smile and said, "Eat up; you're going to need your strength, Hudson."

The way he said it sent a tingle down Hudson's spine right to the end of his tail, and the tingle seemed to escape his tail and fill the cabin with an electric charge. Hudson's whiskers tingled too. The ship moved suddenly and the plates and bowls on the catering tray clanked.

"Not long now, old chap," Perry whispered, closing the door.

What about Emma?

I want to see Emma before...

Before anything happens

Before...

Before I go...

Where am I going?

18.

"Hello," the boy with the glasses said again. His glasses looked like the kind of glasses that only really brainy kids wear. Not that wearing glasses makes you brainy. Emma knew that wasn't true. It was what her teacher at school called a 'cliché' – something that is used so much it becomes, well, a cliché.

The boy had an American accent and there was something familiar about him. He stood there looking at Emma and she sat there – looking at him.

He's like a miniature Morgan Astor Hubbard the Third

Like he's Morgan Astor Hubbard the Third as a kid

A kid from the past

Maybe the boy is a… ghost!

Emma felt a tingle run from the back of head, down her neck, and to the base of her spine. She shivered. It was the kind of thing that happened in stories. Stories about ships on the high seas heading into storms.

"Hello, my name is Morgan Astor Hubbard the Fifth," the boy announced in a way that sounded very well practiced. He reeled off the names as if they were the first line of a riddle.

Emma laughed, more out of relief than amusement. The boy was not a ghost. He was a real boy, and he looked like Morgan Astor Hubbard the Third because he was Morgan Astor Hubbard the Third's grandson.

And clearly, he was a boy who loved ships.

Morgan Five!

That much was clear because, under his arm, he carried a large book about the history of ocean liners. He stared at Emma, and she stared back at him.

And they just stared at each other for what seemed like a very long time. It wasn't an awkward stare, but a curious and natural one.

"And who is this young gentleman," Dad asked when he noticed the strange scene – a boy with glasses with a big book under his arm staring at his daughter and clearly not listening to the great jazz being played by Duke Spellington and his Quartet.

"My name is - Morgan… Astor… "he started to say. Emma sighed.

That's enough with all the names!

"Call him Morgan Five," Emma interrupted.

"That's a funny name," Dad was confused.

"Actually, that *is* what people call me. My family and… my friends." Morgan Five said the word 'friends' with a little hesitation as if…

Maybe he doesn't have many friends

Other people would call him a nerd

I hate the word 'nerd'

That's what they call me at school sometimes…

A Cruise Nerd.

"Morgan Five knows all there is to know about ocean liners," Emma said. She was guessing that he did. No kid would walk around with a big book about old ships under his arm if he didn't know everything there is to know about ocean liners.

"It's my hobby," Morgan nodded.

"A fine hobby, young man. You have something in common with Emma here," Dad said. He looked as if he would rather listen to the music than talk.

Emma stood up and pointed towards the far end of the Atlas Bar where there was an empty booth with a window. "Shall we have a talk about ships over there so Dad can listen to Duke Spellington?"

"That's a very fine idea!" Morgan agreed.

He even talks like his grandfather

He's a miniature Morgan Astor Hubbard the Third

Maybe he's even the image of Morgan Astor Hubbard the Second

There must have been four before this one

Where's the Fourth?

"Are you travelling with your mum and dad?" Emma asked.

"My mom, but not my pa," Morgan replied. He looked sad.

Something must have happened to his dad

No point in asking...

I don't know him well enough... yet.

They sat in the booth and a waiter approached just as they sat down. He recognised Morgan and said, "Good evening, Sir, can I get you and your friend something?"

"Pepsi Max!" Emma said a bit too eagerly.

Morgan looked at her and smiled, "Yes, a Pepsi Max for my friend who is called Emma, and a Ginger Ale for me, please. Thank you very much indeed." Morgan handed the waiter his cruise card, the waiter bowed a little, and turned away to collect the drinks.

"My dog is opposite your cat on the Pet Deck," Morgan said.

"Tad?"

"Yes, Tad. He's a Polish terrier."

"Your grandad told me."

"I just wanted to talk to you because... well, you need to know something," Morgan said. He looked away and started to trace his finger along the edge of the wooden table. The ship was moving more now, and Emma looked out of the window saw how the waves had got stronger, deeper, and were getting darker and bluer as the sun set. The low sun created shadows as the waves peaked and then dropped.

"What do I need to know, Morgan the Fifth? Err, Morgan number five?" Emma said with a smile on her face; deep down she knew what the boy was going to tell her.

"Neither of us are here by accident," Morgan said.

The waiter came and placed the drinks, each on a little white napkin, on the table. He also brought a silver bowl with snacks.

"Ooo crisps," Emma said.

"Those are chips," Morgan corrected her.

"We call them 'crisps' in the UK," Emma explained.

"Ah! Of course."

"That's another Britishism. Your grandad told me that. We say one thing for something, and you say another but the thing itself is the same. It always was and always will be." Emma said – very fast.

Morgan looked surprised. Then he said, "Yes, my grandpa loves to compare American and British idioms."

"Iddie whats?"

"The things you say that don't really mean what the words mean but what you really mean... err..." Morgan got lost in his own words. He looked a little embarrassed.

Emma watched as he frowned and looked as if he were flicking through different parts of his brain to find an example. Then his face brightened, "Ah!"

"Yes... and... ah?" Emma said when Morgan didn't explain.

"I'm over the moon! I'm not really *over the moon* – I'm happy. That's an idiom. Americans and British people use very different ones."

Emma still didn't really understand, but she decided not to ask any questions. She didn't want Morgan to get distracted. She wanted to get to the point.

"I'd better get to the point," he said taking a crisp and tasting it. He munched for a second and then said, "Your cat..."

"Hudson," Emma said.

"Hudson. Yes, your cat Hudson and my dog Tad are onboard for a reason, and it makes me sad, but I know it's what is best for Tad and it's also best for Hudson." Morgan said.

He sat back and sipped his Ginger Ale, and his hand shook a little as if he didn't really believe what he was saying. Not the part about what needed to happen, and what *would* happen, but the part about him accepting it. Deep down he was as sad as Emma was.

They both sat there for a moment, feeling the movement of the ship and sipping their drinks. Neither of them felt queasy but they both felt sad.

"You get used to it, after a while," Morgan said.

"Get used to what?" Emma looked up at Morgan and she could see that he was trying really hard *not* to look upset. In her heart she knew that she would soon have to make choices; the kind she didn't like making.

"To… well… to when something you love very much is gone," Morgan said softly.

"Something?"

"Someone." Morgan pretended he had something in his eye. He rubbed it but Emma could see he was holding back tears.

"Well, if it's what Hudson wants, then it's good for him. And I don't want to stop him doing what he wants to do. What he's always dreamt of doing." Emma tried to keep her voice sounding calm.

Morgan nodded but didn't look up at her.

Then Emma stood up and said, as confidently as she could, "It's time I went to see Hudson then."

With that she turned and left. Morgan Astor Hubbard the Fifth watched her and the tears began tumbling down his cheeks.

19.

The ship was really rocking now. Emma felt the movement beneath her feet as she left the Atlas Bar. She could hear the jazz quartet swinging almost in time to the building storm outside.

As she walked gingerly, her hands instinctively reaching out to grasp the handrails or the wall so she could steady herself, all she could think about was seeing Hudson before...

Before what?

I don't even know what's going to happen

But something is going to happen tonight

Now...

While the storm rages

Emma stopped at the landing where the lifts were. There were stairs going down and stairs going up. On the walls were old paintings of old ships, in calm seas and in rough waters too. They were the kind of paintings that Morgan Five would love. *Did* love. He probably had them at home. His family were obviously really, really rich.

They OWN the ship!

The thought struck her suddenly.

Of course!

They own the ship and that's why they know about…

About what?

About what was going to happen to Hudson?

That's why Morgan Five was so sad about Tad!

Emma knew that time was short. She looked at the deck number. For a moment she'd forgotten where she was. Deck 10. So that meant…

Go up!

She anxiously pressed the button to call the lift. It binged and lit up. But nothing happened.

No time to wait!

Run!

So, she ran up the stairs. She knew that the Pet Deck extended across most of the length of the ship, so it didn't matter whether she was at the aft or the bow – the back or the front – so she just took two steps at a time and focused on getting up where she knew she had to be.

Emma had to pause at the bottom of the last set of stairs because the ship rolled and the entire

landing behind her looked like it was made of jelly -
she laughed as she tried to keep her balance.

*Morgan Five would tell me that in America they
call it Jello.*

Why didn't Morgan Five follow me?

Isn't he going to say goodbye to Tad?

Maybe he has already!

Finally, Emma got to the Pet Deck, and she
pushed at the door.

It was locked!

Nooooo!

She banged on the door, but no one came. She
peered in. It was almost dark. She could see Bingo, the
lemur, jumping and screeching, but she couldn't hear
her.

I need to get in!

Then she remembered that there was a door
from the Pet Promenade Deck. Maybe she could get
in that way.

Emma pushed against the door that led
outside. The wind didn't want her to go out. It pressed
hard against the other side of the door, but Emma put
her shoulder to the wood, and she pushed and
pushed and slowly, very slowly, the door opened, and
she felt the cold force of the wind as it howled like an
army of ghosts flying across the surface of the sea.

Finally she managed to make it outside and had to jump away quickly as the door slammed shut. She knew she'd done a dangerous thing, something she should not have done at all, but this was an emergency.

The sea roared. The wind slammed against every surface. The flags by the huge funnel flapped violently, and the deck itself was wet and slippery.

Emma could see the doors through which the animals were taken for their walks. She had to get there without being blown away. She held on as tight as she could to the metal handrail which was welded firmly onto the Promenade Deck.

Step by step, she got closer and closer. Her dress was soaked with rain and sea foam. Her hair looked like a scarecrow's, and her eyes stung with the wind and the salt from the sea.

Even so. she couldn't help but look out at the ocean. The angry ocean. It was now roiling and boiling and grey and white with streaks of blue. It was moving everywhere. Every drop of water was in motion. The clouds were low and getting thicker and lower and blacker and blacker. The sun had runaway and was sinking below the horizon.

At last she got to the door she pushed and pushed with all her strength and finally it opened. The animals inside reacted as the wind gusted inwards and Emma was almost blown to the floor. For a moment she thought she was flying. The wind was so strong she felt like a leaf being blown down from a tree.

In an instant she was inside, the door slammed shut with a loud, frightening bang that echoed around the Pet Deck. And then suddenly… there was silence.

A surprising silence. All the animals stared at her. She looked like a ghost. Pale and bedraggled with wet hair streaked across her face.

Even Marmaduke woke up looking slightly green, but he was alert now. All the animals seemed to know what was about to happen.

"And what are you doing here?" a voice asked.

It was a human voice, and one she recognised.

"Actually, I think I know why you're here, Emma." It was Morgan Astor Hubbard the Third.

He stood by Hudson's cabin in his elegant, old-fashioned overcoat. Next to him was Chief Pet Officer Perry Petty, smart as ever in his crisp white uniform.

"I told you she'd get here somehow," another familiar voice said. Morgan Five was kneeling by Tad's cage.

How did he get here so fast!

Emma was confused. There was a storm in her brain now as well as outside.

"She's an intrepid young lady," Perry was impressed by Emma's determination.

"I think you deserve an explanation, young lady." Morgan Three beckoned Emma closer. She walked carefully toward Hudson's cabin.

Hudson was sitting calmly, licking his paw. He was cleaning himself. Getting ready.

Ready for what exactly?

"We search high and low for the right animals, the perfect animals for our very special cruise ships," Morgan Three explained.

"Animals who have a special relationship with the sea, even if they don't really know themselves," Perry said.

"But *we always know,*" Morgan Three continued. He placed his hand on Emma's shoulder and then knelt down to be closer to Hudson. Emma did the same.

Hudson looked at her, his eyes bright with excitement and, Emma could tell, just a little fear too. The good kind of fear. The kind that makes you eager to start a new adventure.

"Hudson is a born leader," Morgan Three said. "He was born at sea, and he is destined to spend his life at sea too. Leading others, bringing fun and excitement to children from all over the world."

"But... I mean, what kind of ship could that be? Surely animals can't crew an actual ship... that's impossible!" Emma exclaimed.

"Not in this world, but in another. A world that exists side by side with this one. A world where children can go on a cruise on their own, without any adults, and learn so much and have so much fun. That's the world we're talking about. It's the world we want Hudson to be in. All you have to do is agree. You need to let him go." Morgan Three stood up and peered at Emma. He had a serious, but kind look in his eyes. Emma knew she had to make a decision. She knew that she should let Hudson go.

I want to

But I don't want to...

"It's almost time: We're getting to the critical point in the storm..." Perry said with urgency in his voice.

Emma stared at him for a moment and then looked back at Hudson.

"Leave her alone with him," Morgan Three said and he and Perry moved away.

Hudson and Emma were alone at last.

20.

The ship rocked. The windows rattled. The rain splashed and splished and streaked across the glass. The grey skies were getting greyer and greyer, shading into black as the raindrops collected eager to burst out and dive down toward the sea.

Night was falling. Not just falling but tumbling across the sky. The yellow lights of the Pet Deck made everything seem ghostly, and Hudson's ginger fur looked richer and deeper in its wonderful colours.

"I want to go but I don't want to go," Hudson said, his voice suddenly smaller and less confident than it usually was.

Emma smiled, "That's what I keep saying in my head, I want you to go but I don't want you to go. I really *don't* want you to go."

"I'll stay if you really want me to," Hudson said. He sounded like he meant it, or at least like he wanted Emma to think that he meant it. But Emma knew he didn't really.

"No, you need to go. This is what you were born to do."

"I'll miss you," he said.

"Don't you remember what you said to me that first evening… that evening on the beach in Brighton when you just appeared out of the blue? Don't you remember?" Emma asked.

"I remember. Very clearly."

"You said… something very simple and very easy to understand."

My name's Hudson, and it is my ambition to be the captain of a cruise ship. I am very pleased to meet you.

The words seemed to echo around the Pet Deck as though they'd just come over the speakers in the ceiling. Like it was an announcement from the captain.

Suddenly, there was silence again. The storm seemed to have been put on mute. The other animals were all quiet. It was just Emma and Hudson, together, in a bubble of time.

"I don't want you to leave but if you stay I'll always know that I made you stay, and that would not make me happy," Emma said.

"Somehow there'll be a way to stay in touch," Hudson said confidently.

"There will be, I know it."

"And maybe, just maybe, you'll be able to come on my ship," Hudson said. There was a sudden twinkle in his eyes.

My ship

MY SHIP!

Suddenly the noise of the storm broke through, and the *Magical Seas* rocked again. Outside, a flash of lightning illuminated the angry clouds.

"It's time," Hudson declared, his voice confident and certain now.

He was right. It *was* time. Emma stood up and stepped back. She found Morgan Five standing next to her. He was looking at Tad in the same way that Emma was looking at Hudson. There were tears in everyone's eyes.

Hudson smiled in the way that only Hudson could. Emma waved her hand, but it seemed like such a silly, useless thing to do. It was the only thing she could think of doing.

Flash!

Rolling thunder

Bursts and sparks of lightning

Everything went dark. Emma felt as if she were floating – in the air and in time – and for a moment her ears seemed to fill with water, bubbling, swirling water, but she didn't feel afraid, she felt like she was floating free... and then

Pop!

She was standing in the middle of the Pet Deck and Tad was gone.

Marmaduke was gone.

Kat was gone.

Big Tiny was gone.

Tad was gone and…

And…

AND!

Hudson was gone.

Gone as though he'd never been there. As though this whole voyage had been a dream. Still *was* a dream.

But it wasn't. Emma felt the sting of tears in her eyes but didn't cry. She was happy. Sad and happy. You can be both at the same time. Her mum had told her that. And it was true. *Now* she knew that was true.

She looked into Hudson's empty cat basket. A small cat toy was rolling from one side of it to the other as the ship moved in the storm which was still pounding it from all sides.

There were still some Temptys in his bowl… and a tuft of ginger fur gently floated in a sudden shaft of moonlight that broke through a gap in the angry clouds.

Now Emma knew that…

…a new story was about to begin.

Hudson was gone!

21.

What will Mum and Dad say?

What will I tell them when they discover that Hudson is gone?

They'll miss him so much.

Especially mum.

The storm had passed just as suddenly as it had rolled in from over the horizon. Emma stood on the Promenade Deck, her back against the cool white steel of the ship. She felt safe and surprisingly happy.

She wasn't sad because she knew that Hudson was where he wanted to be, doing what he always wanted to do, but she knew that every day she would think about him.

Each morning when he didn't come in to her room and snuggle into her bedcovers.

Each time the cat-flap flapped in the wind or didn't flap at all.

Each time she was in the supermarket and headed for the pet-food isle to find a packet of Temptys only to stop herself when she realised that she didn't need them anymore. Because Hudson wasn't there.

Each time she stared at the garden fence expecting to see Hudson balanced on top, examining his kingdom.

She still didn't feel sad.

What had happened was meant to be.

Mum chose *this* cruise for a reason. And that reason was simple: it was Hudson's destiny.

Standing in his way would be selfish. Emma sighed deeply. A warm feeling spread across her body. She was happy. For Hudson and for herself. Who knew what adventures he would have and...

Maybe...

just maybe

...what adventures Emma might have in the future.

Emma knew she had to tell Mum and Dad the truth. She took a deep breath, stood away from the ship and was about to go and find them when she spied a magical man in a white suit sitting on one of the deck loungers that were lined up facing the ocean.

"Do you think they could handle the truth?" Peter said. He was playing with a deck of cards and flicking them around and around, moving them from finger to finger and hand to hand in a blur. Emma realised that he really could read minds.

"What choice do I have?" Emma asked.

"You could choose *not* to tell them," Peter said.

"But they'll wonder where Hudson is. They'll think something bad happened to him!"

"Or you could tell them the absolute truth," a mischievous smile spread across Peter's on his face. The kind of smile that meant he didn't believe a word he was saying.

"It's always best to tell the truth," Emma said.

"What if the truth is… it never happened?" Peter asked.

"What do you mean?"

"I can make it that they never knew a cat called Hudson. I can erase him from their memories. It's simple magic, you know, easy stuff." Peter stood up and crossed his arms. The pack of cards he had been playing with had disappeared.

For a moment, Emma didn't believe that Peter could erase her parents' memories. And what about little Brother? He never forgot anything!

Something told her that he *could* actually do it.

That would be awful…

They loved Hudson and it would be horrible to take that love away…

When you've known a cat like Hudson, your life has changed…

...for the better.

NOT knowing him – NEVER having known him... would just be bad.

"No, I'm going to tell them the exact truth," Emma said firmly.

Peter smiled. He looked pleased. "That's the right answer."

"But they still won't actually believe what happened," Emma added.

"Yes, they'll find it very hard to believe," Peter said rubbing his chin with his long fingers.

Suddenly, he stood straight and put his hands up as if he'd just discovered treasure. Only it was the treasure of a great idea.

"How about I suspend their disbelief?" he said.

"What's that?"

"When you watch a film, you *know* it's a film, and you stop looking at the world as if it's real. So people can fly, and cats can talk, aliens regularly visit the Earth and go shopping in Walmart, and you just accept it like it's true. Don't you do that every time you watch TV or a movie?" Peter asked.

"Yes, but..."

"That's when you suspend your disbelief. That makes a story so much more enjoyable. When you *believe* that people can fly, and cats can talk and... all the other unbelievable things that happen in stories,"

Peter watched Emma's face as she worked out exactly what he'd said.

Emma's eyes widened as she realised that maybe, just maybe Peter could really do such a thing.

"So, I'll make sure that's exactly what they do. You tell them the total truth – how Hudson and some of the other animals have been taken into a magical world to be the crew of a cruise ship in another dimension – and they'll just say… 'Oh yes, that's nice, Emma, my darling daughter. Now where shall we eat our dinner?" Peter stood up and took a deep breath.

The breeze was cool, and the sun was close to the horizon. A pink streak was beginning to form in the calm sea.

Emma could hear her mum saying Peter's words, all except the 'darling daughter' bit.

It could work

Why not?

It could work because Emma believed everything that had happened *did* happen. For real. In *her* world.

Yes, it was magic – but it was also REAL.

And Peter was someone who really could do magic.

"OK, let's do it," Emma decided with a big smile.

22.

Mum and Dad were picking up Little Brother from the Kids' Club. He had drawn a picture of sharks circling an alien which was standing on a tiny tropical island with just one palm tree.

"The alien is wondering what those funny fish are with fins because on his planet there's no sea and no fish," Little Brother mused.

Mum looked at the picture with a frown. She always said something nice about Little Brother's pictures, but sometimes she got a little worried by how her son's imagination worked.

"Yes, dear, that's lovely," she said. Then she saw Emma and Peter. "Emma!" she shouted handing the picture back to Little Brother, who frowned.

"Mum, this is Peter. He's the lecturer on the ship and... ummm... well... err..." Emma was about to tell her that Hudson had gone when Peter's soft hand brushed her shoulder, and she stopped talking.

"Nothing's wrong is it?" Mum asked, looking a little worried.

"Nothing's wrong, Emma's mum. Nothing at all. Nothing at all. All is wonderful," Peter said.

There was something soft and musical about the way he was speaking. Peter's eye seemed to shine a little and his tall frame leaned forward just a little. He towered over Mum, and she was instantly enchanted.

Dad suddenly began to pay attention. He'd been looking at his phone, probably checking the football scores. He frowned for a moment and Peter turned towards him, the same soft shine in his eyes, and Dad smiled and put his phone back in his pocket.

"The only thing is, Emma's mum and Emma's dad," Peter said looking from one to the other. "It's just such a little thing, such a magical thing. Well, the truth is, Hudson has been transported into another magical dimension where he has become the captain of a wonderful cruise ship which is crewed by animals and the only passengers are children."

The whole scene froze.

Emma felt a little chill as though the door to the Promenade Deck had been opened and a rush of sea breeze had flowed into the ship. She shivered and imagined she heard the distant tingling of tiny bells, or the gentle patter of sea spray on the windows.

The moment seemed to pass in slow-motion and felt as if it was going to last forever when...

"'Oh yes, that's nice, Emma, my darling daughter. Now where shall we eat our dinner?"

Dear Hudson

I miss you. I guess you know that, but I know you're where you want to be. Where you need to be. Where you SHOULD be.

I miss you.

So so much.

Morgan Astor Hubbard the Fifth told me the secret. And now I understand why they chose you to be captain of a very special cruise ship.

They said you could send me messages. Please send me as many as you can.

I hope they have Temptys where you are - I know it's another world, well, our world but another dimension that only specially chosen kids can visit.

Be safe. Make friends. I know cats don't really make friends, but you're a different kind of cat. You're one of a kind, Hudson, and I know you'll have LOTS of friends on your ship.

I'll write to you as often as I can, and maybe one day, I can come on your ship too.

I hope so. I REALLY hope so.

Miss you. Love you.

Emma xxx

Are you ready to take Captain Hudson's brilliant cruise?

This BOOK is your ticket.

And you need to be adventurous, curious, and ready to try new things

Ready?

Then it's time to embark on brilliant cruise adventures with Captain Hudson!

Captain Hudson's Brilliant Cruise to Alaska

Explore Captain Hudson's ship, *Brilliant Ocean One*, and discover a world where all the crew are animals and the only passengers allowed onboard are kids!

It's great fun onboard and can get a little dangerous ashore as Captain Hudson and his crew venture into the frozen wilds and have an amazing adventure.

Captain Hudson's Brilliant Cruise to the Caribbean

A fast-moving adventure in the brilliant waters of the Caribbean, with everything you expect – pirates, treasure and thrills – as well as a lot of fun surprises.

Captain Hudson's Guide To Brilliant Cruises For Kids

A great guide to everything you have to do to help grown-ups plan a great cruise, great ready for one, and then have a brilliant time when you're onboard the ship. There's lots of space to write stuff down and draw pictures too.

Go to **emmacruises.com** for T-shirts and other great gifts.

You can also see lots of great videos about Emma's cruises and the advice she gives to cruisers of all age ages on Emma's YouTube channel – yes, you guessed it - it's called **emmacruises**

The Authors

Emma Le Teace is one of the world's leading cruise vloggers with millions of views on YouTube. When she was eleven, her parents took her on her first voyage to Alaska. She was immediately enchanted by the experience. After graduating from university with a degree in maths, she got a job in data analysis, but her passion for the sea only got stronger. Emma began sharing her experiences and advice on YouTube and struck a chord with audiences all over the world. Her channel and website, emmacruises.com, has become a valuable source of comment, inspiration, insight and information for both seasoned and novice cruisers.

Jerome Vincent has had a varied career in writing. He's written twenty radio dramas and comedies for the BBC, created a children's TV series, and scripted three series of an animated show called 'Christopher Crocodile.' He's written TV documentaries, a novel about cybercrime, and a feature film. He also writes for heritage sites and museums, including The Tower of London, Kensington Palace, Westminster Abbey, Hampton Court Palace and many more. Jerome's first cruise was the transatlantic crossing on Queen Mary 2.

ACKNOWLEDGEMENTS

A big thank you to Jono, Ruth, Max, Kevan, and Andy for much proofing and editing.

Thanks to Zara, Eliza, Josh, and Noah for your love of Captain Hudson. Your excitement was the inspiration to create this book series.

Rita Ullo and Paul Mulligan for constant insights, advice and editing suggestions.

Peter Croyle for inspiration and the benefit of his vast cruising experience.

Printed in Great Britain
by Amazon

47696079R00086